*Essential Chinese Hot Pot Cookbook*

# *Essential* CHINESE HOT POT COOKBOOK

### Everything you need to enjoy and entertain at home

Jeff Mao

Photography by Darren Muir

ROCKRIDGE
PRESS

Cover Designer: Gabe Nansen
Art Producer: Tom Hood
Editor: Annie Choi
Production Editor: Rachel Taenzler
Production Manager: Riley Hoffman

Photography © Darren Muir, 2021.
Food styling by Yolanda Muir.

Paperback ISBN: 978-1-63807-356-7
eBook ISBN: 978-1-63807-815-9

R0

# Contents

# Introduction and How to Use This Book

*My kitchen is filled with memories—many of them tied to the utensils, pots, and dishes we used for hot pot.* Among them are a collection of brass wire hot pot skimmers from my childhood. Each time I come across one of them, I am brought back to the memory of loading it up with jumbo shrimp and carefully lowering it into the bubbling broth of our traditional charcoal hot pot.

I've been eating hot pot for as long as I can remember, from everyday meals at home to holiday feasts at my grandparents'. Holidays and special occasions have often meant hot pot, but I also love that even a weeknight hot pot feels like an occasion filled with good conversation and good food and not just a meal!

For many years, I lived in the same town as my grandparents, an aunt and uncle, and my cousins. This meant dinner together usually involved going to a restaurant since none of us wanted to cook for 8 to 10 people. However, hot pot offered an easy alternative. It allowed us to gather the whole family and easily manage the vegetarians and meat eaters of the family, and it took very little time in the kitchen. There's certainly some prep work, but nothing like a Chinese meal for 10 that would have necessitated at least 8 to 10 entrées! I loved making my sauce—hot and spicy with a touch of vinegar—to satisfy my need for heat while others didn't have to contend with it if they didn't want to.

Whether you are brand-new to hot pot or a seasoned hot pot lover, you'll find plenty of broth and sauce recipes and delicious combinations to try in this book. Hosting your hot pot gathering requires some setup, but nothing too complicated. The broth that you choose for your hot pot can be a simple store-bought chicken broth, or you can make your own from scratch, rich with flavors characteristic of a region of China. Likewise, what you choose to cook in your hot pot can be an exercise in cleaning out your refrigerator, or it can be a carefully curated grouping of foods. In this book, I've crafted recipes inspired by authentic regional traditions as well as provided you with simple delicious options using ingredients found in any conventional grocery store.

Since hot pot is an occasion, a way of cooking, and a meal, I've organized this book to help you get the most out of your hot pot experience. Chapter 2 covers everything from selecting your hot pot equipment and setting it up to understanding what you can cook in your hot pot. Chapters 3 and 4 cover recipes to make the broth and dipping sauces. Finally, we'll bring it all together in chapters 5 and 6, where you'll get pairings of broth, sauces, and ingredients inspired by different regions of China. Let's get started—it's hot pot time!

# CHAPTER ONE

# Essential Chinese Hot Pot

A successful hot pot gathering at home requires some simple but necessary equipment and a little planning. In this chapter, we'll cover the equipment, the setup, and all the details about hosting a hot pot meal.

# ALL ABOUT CHINESE HOT POT

Chinese hot pot (huǒguō, 火锅) isn't a single dish. It is both an occasion and a way of cooking. Think of it as the Chinese version of the classic American barbecue. Asking friends to your home for barbecue doesn't tell them exactly what's on the menu, but everyone will expect a grill, a fun social gathering, and most likely beer. Chinese hot pot is very much the same, but the cooking is done in a flavorful broth simmering at your table instead of over a grill.

At Chinese hot pot, everyone including kids cooks their own food, which ranges from thinly sliced meats, Chinese greens, and seafood to mushrooms and noodles. It usually includes beer (at least for the adults), and everyone has their own take on the dipping sauce that they use to dress up their meal.

The broth imbues the ingredients you cook in it with flavor, so it's foundational to any hot pot meal. Not only will you find seafood-, chicken-, beef-, pork-, or mutton-based broths, but you'll also find vegetarian ones like mushroom- or herb-based broths. It is common to have two broths at one hot pot: one spicy, one not. The contrast follows the Chinese tenet of balance, yin and yang. In fact, you can purchase a hot pot pan that has a divider to serve the two broths in a single pot in the yin and yang shape.

In many hot pot restaurants, there are specially designed tables with built-in heating elements that will keep the broth simmering. The long menu may look intimidating, but it's much simpler than it appears. Many restaurants offer pre-selected combinations of meats, vegetables, and noodles to make ordering easier, but you can also order à la carte. Either way, there are just three essential steps: choose a broth, choose the ingredients, and make your dipping sauce at the sauce bar (think salad bar). At the sauce bar, you grab a bowl, choose a sauce base (or mix a few), and add aromatics. Then simply place some meat or vegetables into the simmering broth and allow them to cook. You'll get a small personal strainer to help you add and remove the food from the hot broth. When the food is cooked, dip it in your sauce and enjoy. Repeat, and order more plates of ingredients as needed!

Of course, good food knows no boundaries. Hot pot is also common in Taiwan, Korea, and Japan and across Southeast Asia, too. Thailand's signature *Tom Yum* broth is both sour and spicy and is flavored with lemongrass, galangal, lime leaves, and bird's-eye chile peppers. Japanese hot pot (called *shabu shabu*) is traditionally a very mild kelp-based broth. Besides the variation on broths, what really sets Chinese hot pot apart is the salad bar approach to the dipping sauces. I've seen dipping sauce bars in Beijing that had at least 20 different sauces, aromatics, oils, and other ingredients available for you to make your dipping sauce exactly how you like it!

## Hot Pot History

There are countless stories about the origins of hot pot, many of which attribute it to Mongolian invaders cooking in their helmets. However, hot pot is Chinese in origin. Ancient bronze hot pot vessels dating to the Han Dynasty (202 BCE–220 CE) survive, which strongly suggests that the Chinese had been enjoying hot pot for over 1,000 years before the Mongol invasion of China.

## Hot Pot Today

Hot pot is now enjoyed all over the Asia-Pacific region and beyond. China's largest hot pot restaurant chains, Haidilao and Little Sheep (aka Happy Lamb Hot Pot in the United States), have locations throughout China and the Asia-Pacific region as well as locations in the United States, Canada, Europe, and Africa! Fondue, usually attributed to Switzerland, is not the same as hot pot. *Fondue* comes from the French word *fondre*, which means "to melt." Most commonly, fondue is melted cheese with wine or melted chocolate. The Swiss use their fondue pots to do Chinese hot pot, but they call it *la fondue chinoise*, or literally "Chinese fondue."

## SOCIALIZING OVER SOUP

Unlike other meals where food is cooked in the kitchen and everyone is served at the table together, hot pot meals involve cooking the food throughout the meal at the table and eating as the food becomes ready. This process necessarily creates some downtime, and that's okay. Hot pot is a social occasion where you're encouraged to sit back, relax, and enjoy the conversation while you cook your dinner, one small bite at a time. Pace yourself! While it may seem like you aren't eating that much food, I've never known anyone to walk away from hot pot without a full belly.

## Regional Differences

China has numerous regional cuisines that have evolved over thousands of years. In this book, I'll include flavor profiles from all over China. The broth varies, while your ingredients or the foods that you cook in the hot pot broth are mostly the same. Lamb-based broths are common, especially in northern China, but broths based on other meat or seafood can be found, including some distinctive regional specialties like the mushroom broth from Yunnan province or the sour fish broth of Guizhou province. The most popular broth across all of China is the Sichuan-style broth, which is known for its signature numbing and spicy hot qualities, called *Ma La* (麻辣). The city of Chongqing, with about 16 million people in Sichuan province, is the hot pot capital of the planet, with a hot pot restaurant for every 607 residents! For comparison, New York City has a Starbucks for every 35,778 residents.

# MOST POPULAR HOT POT BROTHS

### Sichuan Red Ma La Broth (page 38):

Often served in a split pot with another mild, non-spicy broth. Originally from Sichuan province, it is popular all over China.

### Mandarin Duck Clear Broth (page 39):

A mild broth that is frequently paired with a spicy Sichuan Red Ma La Broth.

### Tomato Broth (page 62):

Tomato broth is a flavorful vegan broth that is sometimes also made with chicken or pork broth. It's popular all over China.

### Mandarin Lamb Broth (page 49):

A simple mild broth made from lamb that is popular in northern and western China.

### Yunnan Mushroom Broth (page 46):

An earthy, flavorful broth. Yunnan province is famous for its wild mushrooms. Mushroom broth is available and popular all over China, but in Yunnan province, you will find unique flavors from wild mushrooms only found and available locally.

# MAKING CHINESE HOT POT AT HOME

· · · · · · · · · · · · · · · · · · ·

Hosting hot pot at home can be an easy way to feed a large group. It requires hot pot equipment, some organization, and just a little bit of prep work. In this section, you'll get an overview of the essential hot pot equipment and how to set it all up.

## Choosing a Hot Pot Setup

To make hot pot, you need a stand-alone heat source and a pot unless you choose an option with a pot built in. Here are some ways to set up a hot pot at home:

### COUNTERTOP BURNERS

Countertop burners have a heating element like a regular stove. You'll find electric radiant heat coils, glass-top infrared, and cast-iron plate burners as well as induction and butane (gas) burner styles. Whichever you choose, it should be large enough that your hot pot pan does not extend over the controls. (You don't want to burn yourself trying to adjust the temperature.) Electric models should have automatic shutoff safety features and clear indicators when they are powered on. Quality countertop burners are readily available in all styles at the $35 to $85 range.

**ELECTRIC RADIANT HEAT:** Often called hot plates, these produce enough heat for hot pot, unlike a warming plate. An electric burner should be rated 1200+ watts to easily boil broth. Infrared burners are the most efficient, can change temperature quickly, and are the easiest to clean.

**INDUCTION BURNERS:** More efficient than radiant heat types, these use electromagnetic induction to heat the pan directly. They don't heat your room nearly as much as all other countertop burner styles, which is beneficial if you live in a warm climate. If you choose an induction burner, remember that your cooking pot must be magnetic. A magnet should stick firmly to the pot.

**BUTANE BURNERS:** Portable butane stoves are light and easy to situate on any table anywhere since they lack a power cord. There is no trip hazard, either! They provide quick and flexible temperature control, but they can noticeably heat your room. Plus, you must purchase consumable butane fuel cans. A can costs about $2 to $3 and lasts about 3 to 4 hours.

## HOT POT PANS

If you use a countertop burner, you'll need a separate hot pot pan. Generally, a pot should be wide and shallow as opposed to tall and deep so that you can see into it while seated and you won't lose food at the bottom of the pot. Options range from $20 to $60, but you may already have the perfect pot in your kitchen.

**SPLIT OR SINGLE POT:** Unlike a single pot that cooks only one broth, a split pot lets you cook with two broths (usually one spicy, one not). Split versions are available in either soldered or cast. The soldering often leaves markings on the outside of the pan that some people don't care for. These can be prone to leaking between the two broths and rust at the solder points. A cast pan is one solid piece, usually made from aluminum with a nonstick coating. These won't leak or rust, but make sure they are perfluorooctanoic acid (PFOA)-free.

**WESTERN-STYLE COOKING POTS:** Whether you are purchasing a new pot or looking at your current cookware, look for a pot that is 10 to 14 inches in diameter and 2½ to 4 inches in height with a 4- to 5-quart capacity.

## ALL-IN-ONE HOT POTS

All-in-one hot pots are appliances with an integrated heating element and pot, which means there's no need for a separate pot. Some are designed specifically for hot pot. Other usable options may be called a combo cooker.

**ELECTRIC HOT POT:** These all-in-one appliances ($30 to $130) are specifically designed for hot pot and are available as a single-broth cooking pot or split. Some include a grill component for Korean barbecue. Make sure that the cooking vessel detaches from the electric heating element for easy cleaning.

**CHARCOAL HOT POT:** You can still find and purchase hot pots made in the traditional style, but they are more expensive ($125 to $300), and I would only use them outdoors. Also, make sure to place them on a heat-proof surface just in case hot coals fall onto the base plate.

**FONDUE POT:** Designed for cheese or chocolate fondue, electric fondue pots can work. Look for "broth fondue" or "la fondue chinoise" on the packaging or product descriptions. Most fondue pots are smaller (1 to 2 quarts) than most hot pot appliances (3 to 6 quarts). If you are planning to cook for more than two people, then I'd recommend a different setup.

**INSTANT POT OR MULTI-COOKER:** A functional option, but not recommended because most common electric pressure cookers ($70 to $170) have tall sides and a deep cooking pot. You have to rise from your chair to see inside, and that's awkward and tiring! Temperature control can be more challenging, too.

**SLOW COOKER:** Not recommended because slow cookers typically only have two settings, low and high, making temperature control difficult.

## Getting the Most Out of Your Hot Pot

To make your hot pot setup last, follow the manufacturer's instructions for cleaning and care. To get the most out of it, remember that while not all fondue pots can hot pot, all hot pots can fondue! They also work well for other large family gatherings like Thanksgiving when you need to keep food warm on a buffet.

## Other Essential Equipment

**BOWLS:** A small rice bowl is all you really need. It should be large enough to mix your dipping sauce in and dip your food into but small enough to hold in your hand.

**CHOPSTICKS:** The traditional eating utensil in most East Asian cultures, they make it easier than a fork to pluck a morsel of food from the hot pot. I recommend bamboo or wood chopsticks over plastic or metal. Plastic can melt if you touch a hot surface, and metal can get hot enough to burn your mouth.

**HOT POT STRAINERS:** Sometimes called spider strainers, these are made especially for hot pot and have a long handle with a small basket. Use them to lower ingredients into the hot pot to cook in the basket rather than dropping in ingredients and splashing hot broth.

**KNIFE AND CUTTING BOARD:** You shouldn't need these at the table since all of the ingredients should be pre-cut into bite-size servings. If your friends or family will be helping prepare the ingredients, having extra knives and boards is helpful! If you have young kids, you might even consider getting a plastic vegetable knife. They are available for under $10 and can easily cut greens like Chinese cabbage or bok choy.

**LADLES:** A ladle will help you serve the broth when eaten as a soup. You only need one for each hot pot at the table.

**PLATES:** Table space can be at a premium, so use small plates instead of large dinner plates.

**SLOTTED SPOONS:** Some hot pots will come with personal-size slotted spoons to help you retrieve ingredients from the broth. Typically, their shape doesn't hold on to ingredients like a hot pot strainer.

**TONGS:** Tongs can help retrieve cooked foods like noodles. They can also transfer raw meat and seafood to the hot pot. Keep one pair for each plate so there is no cross-contamination. Mini tongs, ice tongs, or sugar cube tongs work well.

## Nice-to-Haves

A lid for your hot pot decreases the time it takes to bring the broth to a boil. Baby spoons are great for the sauce bar. They make it easy to add small amounts of ingredients.

# SETTING UP AND USING YOUR HOT POT

Since you will be cooking at the table, you want to make sure that your setup is safe and easy to use. For electric hot pots, arrange the cord so that it isn't a trip hazard. If you have small children who are likely to get up and wander during the meal, this is especially important. For butane burners, make sure your room is well ventilated.

## SETTING THE TABLE

Set up a sauce and beverage bar on a separate table or counter. Bowls and glasses can be here. The first order of business for your guests is to get a bowl and mix their sauce. They can get a drink, too, and then be seated.

## KEEP THE MEAT AND VEGGIES SEPARATE

As you prep the ingredients before the meal, arrange the meats and vegetables on separate plates to prevent any cross-contamination. Also, keep plates of raw meats and seafood covered in plastic wrap and refrigerate until just before the meal.

## PAY ATTENTION TO COOKING TIME

Different foods take different amounts of time to cook, and some foods don't do as well when overcooked as others. See chapter 2 (page 17) for more on cooking times for each ingredient.

## ADJUSTING THE HEAT

As you add ingredients to your hot pot, the temperature will naturally drop as heat is absorbed by the ingredients. If you notice that the broth has stopped simmering, you can turn up the heat a little to help the broth return to a simmer faster. If the broth comes to a rolling boil, turn the heat down so that it isn't splashing or spitting hot broth and making a mess, or worse, burning someone.

## ADD A LITTLE AT A TIME

Add only those ingredients that you are ready to eat. You don't want to overcrowd the hot pot and drop the temperature too much. You'll be surprised how easy it is for your eyes to be hungrier than your stomach!

# HOT POT FAQ

**Q: Can you drink the broth?**

A: It depends on the broth. The hot, spicy varieties are not typically eaten as soup. It's totally up to you! I like tasting the broth as it changes flavor throughout a meal.

**Q: How much sauce should I use?**

A: One of the best parts of Chinese hot pot is that you are in control of your sauce! Use as much or as little as you like.

**Q: Is it okay to mix the sauces?**

A: Yes, go for it! In chapter 4, I'll show you how to make some classic dipping sauces and sauce bases, but feel free to make your own. At many hot pot restaurants, the sauce bar has dozens of ingredients to mix and match to create your secret sauce.

**Q: What if the broth gets low?**

A: The broth recipes in chapter 3 are usually enough for four to six people. When you start your hot pot meal, you won't use all the broth. I've anticipated that you will need to add more broth as the meal progresses, so you'll want to keep the extra broth warming on the stove. If you run out completely, you can add hot water.

**Q: How do I know when ingredients are cooked through?**

A: The time it takes varies depending on the ingredient. More specifics are in chapter 2, but generally, meatballs, fish balls, and dumplings tend to float when they are cooked. If you have shaved or very thinly cut meats, those require only 10 to 15 seconds of cooking. Some ingredients like certain vegetables are fine to eat without too much cooking, so you are mostly warming them up to taste.

**Q: Is there hot pot etiquette or a special order?**

A: Yes and no. Here are some general guidelines, but with friends and family, there are no rules other than food safety rules!

- For raw meat, use the tongs, not your chopsticks. And don't mix the tongs—the tongs with the chicken are for the chicken!

- Don't steal someone else's foods from the hot pot, but do help eat orphaned and lost food found loose in the pot!

- Add ingredients to simmering broth. Wait if the broth is not boiling.

- Before adding more broth or water, ask if anyone wants some broth first, since the flavor will change with the addition.

- In general, start with ingredients that take longer to cook like root vegetables. Then move on to meats and other vegetables. Noodles often come later.

- Avoid leafy green vegetables in a hot, spicy broth. They pick up a lot of the hot oil and get really spicy because they have so much surface area.

# ENTERTAINING WITH HOT POT

Whether it's just your immediate family or a group of friends, hot pot should be an easy meal. Except for the broth, there is very little cooking to be done beforehand. You can even enlist your friends to help chop and prep plates of ingredients before the meal begins! If you are pressed for time, you can purchase pre-made broth spice packets in a variety of flavors online or at a local Asian market. Just add water!

## Setting Up for Your Hot Pot Party

Most hot pots are large enough to support eight diners. However, eight diners likely can't sit at a table and all reach the hot pot. If that's the case, you need more than one hot pot. Everyone should be able to reach the hot pot from their seat! And if you need more than one hot pot, you also need more than one of each ingredient plate.

I would recommend setting up a separate sauce and beverage station in the kitchen or a sideboard. As with the ingredients on the table, if you have lots of options for making sauces for your guests, make sure each bowl or jar has a dedicated spoon.

If you are feeling stressed out, take a deep breath and delegate! Hot pot is a group activity. Everyone can help with the prep work. Remember, the only advanced cooking that you're likely to do is creating the broth, and that can be done a day or more ahead of time.

## Have Fun!

By now, I hope you've got an idea about the equipment and the basic setup. While there are lots of options, remember that you're basically boiling water. In the next chapter, we'll cover everything you need to know to stock up on hot pot ingredients.

# CHAPTER TWO

# Ingredients for Chinese Hot Pot

In this chapter, I'll help you find and prepare some of the most popular hot pot ingredients along with providing guidance on how long to cook them. Some ingredients may be harder to find than others, but most are common ingredients that you eat regularly.

# WHERE AND HOW TO SHOP

· · · · · · · · · · · · · · · · · · · ·

If you don't live near an Asian grocery store, not to worry! You can do a hot pot meal with ingredients found entirely in a conventional grocery store. If you are hoping to re-create more authentic flavors, though, access to an Asian grocery or online specialty stores will help.

When shopping in an Asian grocery store, you will find the English labels on packaging frequently lack detail or accuracy. I've included the Chinese characters for certain ingredients to help you match them to what you find in a store. See the Resources on page 127 for more information on where to find ingredients.

## If You Don't Have Easy Access to an Asian Grocery Store . . .

Try natural foods stores, which sometimes stock a surprising number of Asian sauces, condiments, and fermented foods. Farmers' markets tend to have a better selection of mushrooms and Asian vegetables.

Finding ingredients for broths and sauces can be more challenging. Fortunately, the Internet has made it easier to access ingredients from all corners of the planet. Here are some shelf-stable ingredients that might be easier to buy online or via Amazon:

→ Sichuan broad bean chili paste (Píxiàn dòubàn jiàng, 郫县豆瓣酱)
→ Red and green Sichuan peppercorns
→ Sa cha sauce (sometimes spelled "sha cha," shā chá jiàng, 沙茶酱)
→ Sichuan dried chili flakes
→ Dried shiitake mushrooms
→ Dried Chinese red dates
→ Red fermented bean curd (hóng fǔrǔ, 紅腐乳)

# STARTING WITH THE BROTH

· · · · · · · · · · · · · · ·

Hot pot broth is one of the few things that you'll need to prepare in advance. While stocks are made from bones and broths are made from meat and/or vegetables, for simplicity, I'll use the term *broth* to refer to both in this book. Here are some different options for preparing hot pot broths.

## Powdered Broth and Seasoning Packets

You can find pre-packaged hot pot broth mixes online or at Asian grocery stores. These are helpful if you want to try out a new flavor before investing in new ingredients that you may not use again. Like canned soup, you simply add water according to the package instructions. Some of the most popular hot pot broth mixes are made by Lee Kum Kee, Haidilao, Little Sheep, and Baijia.

You can also find pre-made broth in cans, concentrates, and bouillon cubes or powder. I like Better Than Bouillon's concentrates. They last a long time in the refrigerator, and you can easily adjust the salt and intensity of the broth by varying how much concentrate you use.

## Fish- or Meat-Based Broth

Meat broths can be made from bones, including discarded bones from a roast, so the next time you eat a rotisserie chicken or cook a bone-in roast of some sort, freeze the bones in a zip-top bag for making broth later. When starting with uncooked bones, the traditional process includes pre-soaking, blanching, browning, and then a long simmer. Fish and seafood bones don't need pre-soaking, and they don't require as long of a simmer.

## Vegetarian and Vegan Broths

Most vegetable scraps can be used to make a broth. While it is traditional in Western cooking to avoid using cruciferous vegetables like cabbage or broccoli in broth since they may add bitter notes, in some hot pot broths, bitterness is part of the goal. If you don't like bitterness, simply serve these vegetables on the table to cook with and not as a broth-flavoring agent. Vegetable broths tend to be faster to make than meat broths.

## Adjusting Seasoning and Flavoring

Many Chinese recipes are based on fermented condiments, like fermented bean curd and Sichuan broad bean chili paste, which often bring a salty and funky flavor. Anchovy paste, tomato paste, and Worcestershire sauce are good substitutes when you need an umami boost. If you know you are sensitive to spicy, sour, or salty foods, start with less. You can always add more spice, but taking it away isn't so easy!

## Keep It Spicy (or Don't)

Most of the heat in spicy hot pot broths comes from dried chile peppers, common in Sichuan-style Ma La broth. For an authentic taste, buy dried lantern (dēnglóng làjiāo, 灯笼辣椒), facing heaven (cháotiān làjiāo, 朝天辣椒), or Sichuan (èr jīngtiáo làjiāo, 二荆条辣椒) chiles. If you can't find Chinese varieties, you can use Mexican varieties like habanero, chiles de arbol, or cayenne. The Ma La broths also have a unique mouth-numbing quality from the Sichuan peppercorns. You'll find a handful of spicy recipes in this book, but there are many other milder recipes that are just as flavorful. Use split pots to serve both spicy and non-spicy broth at the table to give guests a break from the heat. You can also use a split pot to have a vegetarian and non-vegetarian broth to accommodate dietary needs and preferences. Be mindful when cooking leafy greens and blocks of tofu in the spicy broth since they get saturated with spicy oil, making them spicier than other ingredients.

# SAUCES AND VINEGARS

· · · · · · · · · · · · · · · · · · ·

The sauce for your hot pot is key, and you get to make your own! Most of the pre-made sauces you find in an Asian grocery store are not used on their own but form the basis of your sauce. In chapter 4, you'll find some classic sauce combinations and a couple of my personal favorites to help you get started. Here are some of the common sauce bases and condiments:

**CHINESE SESAME PASTE:** Made from ground toasted sesame seeds, Chinese sesame paste (zhīmajiàng, 芝麻酱) comes in jars that have a thick layer of oil on top. Make sure to stir it in like you do with peanut butter. You can substitute tahini with some adjustments (see page 68).

**HOISIN SAUCE:** Commonly thought of as a Chinese barbecue sauce, it adds a sweet, tangy flavor.

**RICE VINEGAR AND CHINESE BLACK VINEGAR:** Rice vinegar is a little sweeter and less acidic than plain white vinegar. Avoid seasoned rice vinegar, as it has both salt and sugar in it. Chinese black vinegar is as dark as soy sauce, is made from fermented black sticky rice, and has a more earthy, malty flavor. Chinese people tend to use black vinegar more frequently for dipping

sauces, and the most popular among them is Zhenjiang (or "Chinkiang") vinegar.

**SA CHA SAUCE:** Although often labeled "barbecue sauce," sa cha sauce is nothing like an American barbecue sauce. Made from brill fish and dried shrimp, it is a popular base for hot pot dipping sauce.

**SOY SAUCE:** The most commonly known Chinese sauce. For your dipping sauces, regular soy sauce (often referred to as light soy sauce) is a good place to start as a base.

**TOASTED SESAME OIL:** Deeply fragrant, toasted sesame oil is heavily used in Sichuan province as the basis of a dipping sauce. Since the spicy flavor compounds in chile peppers are oil-soluble, sesame oil helps absorb the heat.

The black vinegar, sesame paste, and sa cha sauce will most likely require a trip to an Asian grocery or an online purchase.

# INGREDIENTS

In this section, you'll get an overview of ingredients that can be cooked in the hot pot broth. For every ingredient, you'll find helpful information, like about how long it takes to cook in the hot pot and how to prepare it.

## *Tofu and Soy*

Tofu has a mild flavor on its own, so it takes on flavor well from both the broth and your dipping sauce. You'll find most of these ingredients in an Asian grocery store.

### TOFU BLOCKS

For hot pot, extra-firm and firm tofu are best, as they hold their shape.

**COOK TIME:** 3 to 4 minutes

**TO PREP:** Drain and cut into ¾- to 1-inch cubes. You can also freeze, thaw, and press tofu blocks before cutting. This will improve the tofu's ability to soak up flavor from the broth and sauces.

### TOFU SKIN

Tofu skin has a slightly chewy texture and neutral flavor. Look for fresh in the refrigerator or freezer sections; it is also available dried. Sometimes you can also find tofu skin that has been deep fried into crispy square chips.

**COOK TIME:** 1 to 2 minutes

**TO PREP:** If using fresh, simply cut into bite-size pieces or noodles. Dried tofu needs to soak briefly in water to rehydrate it before cutting. Deep-fried versions require no preparation.

### BEAN CURD STICK

These are packaged dried and found in a center aisle of an Asian grocery. Once rehydrated, they have a slightly chewy texture and neutral taste, but the crinkly texture traps flavors from broth and sauce.

**COOK TIME:** 1 to 2 minutes

**TO PREP:** Pre-soak for 8 to 10 hours in cold water; then cut into 2-inch pieces.

## TOFU KNOTS

Look for these packaged dried in a center aisle of an Asian grocery.

**COOK TIME:** 2 to 3 minutes

**TO PREP:** Pre-soak for 20 minutes in room-temperature water.

## FRIED BEAN CURD

Sometimes labeled as soy puffs, these are light and airy with a bit of chew and can be found in the refrigerator section. No prep needed.

**COOK TIME:** 1 to 2 minutes

## Noodles

Noodles are added to the hot pot late in the meal so the noodles cook in the broth after it has been flavored with all the meats and vegetables. For hot pot, stick with lo mein noodles since chow mein noodles are intended to be stir-fried. Choose your desired thickness and type of starch. Most types are sold fresh as well as dried, like spaghetti.

## LO MEIN

A wheat noodle made both with and without egg. Shapes range from very thin to wide, flat noodles.

**COOK TIME:** 3 to 4 minutes (fresh) and 6 to 7 minutes (dried)

**TO PREP:** If frozen, defrost in the refrigerator for 4 to 6 hours; otherwise, none.

## WONTON NOODLES

A wheat noodle that is made from the same dough as wonton wrappers. Usually found fresh or frozen, but not dried.

**COOK TIME:** 3 to 4 minutes

**TO PREP:** If frozen, defrost in the refrigerator for 4 to 6 hours; otherwise, none.

## RAMEN

They have a springy, chewier texture. You can discard the powdered soup mix. No prep needed.

**COOK TIME:** 4 to 5 minutes

## RICE NOODLES

Most commonly sold dried, rice noodles are also available in sizes ranging from very thin noodles to wide, flat noodles. They are good if you are avoiding gluten.

**COOK TIME:** 2 to 4 minutes

**TO PREP:** Follow package instructions. In general, pre-soak the noodles in hot water for 30 minutes or parboil them for 1 minute; then drain.

## MUNG BEAN NOODLES

A very thin, translucent noodle with a slippery texture. They're often called glass noodles.

**COOK TIME:** 1 to 2 minutes

**TO PREP:** Pre-soak in warm water until pliable for 15 to 20 minutes.

## TOFU NOODLES

A noodle cut from thick tofu skin. Sold fresh or frozen. No prep needed.

**COOK TIME:** 1 to 2 minutes

## SHOULD I MAKE MY OWN NOODLES?

Making noodles isn't as hard as it sounds, but it can be time-consuming. If you enjoy the process and you have the time, homemade noodles like Handmade Lo Mein Noodles (page 80) will always taste better than dried. You can also freeze the noodles, and they will cook up fine another day. With some planning, you can have homemade noodles with your hot pot! Now many American grocery stores also stock fresh Italian pasta. While not exactly the same as Chinese noodles, they are a good substitute. If you can find only instant ramen noodles, then use them. They are a perfectly good noodle for hot pot.

# Leafy and Cruciferous Vegetables

Any vegetable with a robust stem and leaves, like chard, collard greens, and kale, works well for hot pot. Here are vegetables traditionally enjoyed with hot pot.

## CHINESE CABBAGE

Also referred to as Napa cabbage.

**COOK TIME:** 1 to 2 minutes for the leafy ends; 2 to 3 minutes for the stalk

**TO PREP:** Separate the leaves; then chop into 1-inch strips across the stalk.

## BOK CHOY

Bok choy has a neutral to slightly bitter flavor, and the thick stalks provide a great crunch. Baby bok choy and dwarf bok choy have a sweeter flavor and are more tender.

**COOK TIME:** 1 to 2 minutes for the leafy parts; 2 to 3 minutes for thick stalks and dwarf bok choy

**TO PREP:** Separate the leaves of bok choy and baby bok choy; then chop into 1-inch strips across the stalk. Quarter the dwarf bok choy lengthwise.

## CHINESE BROCCOLI

Long green stems with large leaves and sometimes with small florets and tiny yellow flowers, Chinese broccoli has a mild sweet flavor.

**COOK TIME:** 1 to 2 minutes for the leafy ends; 2 to 3 minutes for the stems

**TO PREP:** Cut into 2-inch pieces.

## CHOY SUM

With long green stems and large leaves, choy sum has a slightly sweet flavor and a texture like bok choy.

**COOK TIME:** 1 to 2 minutes for the leafy ends; 2 to 3 minutes for the stems

**TO PREP:** Cut into 1-inch pieces.

## TATSOI

The dark green crinkled leaves of tatsoi have a pleasant, sweet flavor.

**COOK TIME:** 1 to 2 minutes for the leafy ends; 2 to 3 minutes for the stems

**TO PREP:** Trim the leaves from the stalk. Cut stalks into 1- to 2-inch pieces.

## SPINACH

Buy mature spinach, often sold in bunches. The baby spinach leaves that are sold for salad won't hold up to boiling.

**COOK TIME:** 10 to 20 seconds

**TO PREP:** Trim the tips of the stalks. Wash and dry thoroughly to remove grit.

# *Mushrooms*

Available fresh and dried, mushrooms add a meaty, earthy flavor to any hot pot. Dried mushrooms tend to have a more pronounced flavor with a chewier texture than fresh. Rehydrate dried mushrooms by soaking them in hot water for 10 to 30 minutes. If using fresh, look for dry, plump mushrooms that are not wilted, wet, or slimy.

## CHINESE BLACK OR SHIITAKE

These mushrooms are common in Chinese cuisine. They have a savory, earthy flavor.

**COOK TIME:** 2 to 3 minutes (dried); 3 to 4 minutes (fresh)

**TO PREP:** Trim the woody stems.

## ENOKI

With long, thin white stalks and small white caps, enoki mushrooms have a delightful crunch and a flavor reminiscent of lobster or shrimp. Fresh is better than dried.

**COOK TIME:** 2 to 3 minutes

**TO PREP:** Trim the ends of the stalks and separate into small clusters by hand.

## SHIMEJI (HON-SHIMEJI)

Also called beech mushrooms, shimeji have white stalks and small brown or white caps. Fresh is better than dried.

**COOK TIME:** 2 to 3 minutes

**TO PREP:** Trim the ends of the stalks to separate into small clusters by hand.

## OYSTER MUSHROOMS

Usually white to gray stems with a gray or beige cap, oyster mushrooms have a nice chewy texture.

**COOK TIME:** 2 to 3 minutes (dried); 3 to 4 minutes (fresh)

**TO PREP:** Trim the ends of the stalks and separate into small clusters by hand.

## WOOD EAR MUSHROOMS

Texture is as important in Chinese cuisine as flavor. Sometimes called tree ear mushrooms, these dark brown leaflike mushrooms have a neutral flavor but provide a crunch unlike any other mushroom. They're most commonly sold dried.

**COOK TIME:** 2 to 3 minutes

**TO PREP:** If dried, pre-soak in warm water for 10 to 15 minutes. Cut into bite-size pieces.

## KING TRUMPET MUSHROOMS

Large mushrooms that are mostly stem. Get fresh when you can find them.

**COOK TIME:** 2 to 3 minutes

**TO PREP:** Cut into ½-inch coins and cross-hatch one side.

# Root and Other Vegetables

Root vegetables do a good job of absorbing flavor from your broth. Aside from the daikon radish, all vegetables oxidize and turn brown or gray when cut, so place cut pieces in a bowl of water and add a tablespoon of vinegar. Drain just before serving.

## LOTUS ROOT

Long and cylindrical, lotus root has smooth pale skin. The white interior has a pinwheel flower pattern of holes. Slightly sweet, lotus root has a crisp texture even when cooked.

**COOK TIME:** 4 to 5 minutes

**TO PREP:** Peel and cut into discs about ⅛ to ¼ inch thick.

## DAIKON RADISH

Often a foot or longer, daikon has a mild flavor. Look for ones with a firm exterior and no soft spots.

**COOK TIME:** 5 to 8 minutes. Cubes take longer than discs to cook through.

**TO PREP:** Peel and then cut into ½-inch-thick discs or 1-inch cubes.

## TARO ROOT

With a ringed, fuzzy exterior, taro root is white and often mottled with beige or pink flecks on the inside. Taro has a nutty, creamy flavor. When fresh, taro should feel heavy for its size.

**COOK TIME:** 15 to 20 minutes until soft like a cooked potato

**TO PREP:** Peel and then rinse with cold water. Cut into ½-inch discs.

## SWEET POTATO

Any sweet potato is good, but American varieties tend to be sweeter than Asian ones.

**COOK TIME:** 6 to 7 minutes

**TO PREP:** Wash well or peel; then cut into ½-inch discs or 1-inch cubes.

## POTATO

Yukon Gold and Red Bliss potatoes hold up best to boiling, but you can use any variety.

**COOK TIME:** 8 to 12 minutes

**TO PREP:** Wash well or peel; then cut into ½-inch discs or 1-inch cubes.

## PUMPKIN AND SQUASH

My favorites for hot pot are butternut, kabocha, sugar pumpkin, delicata, and acorn. These are easy to peel as compared to many squashes that are roasted with the skin on and then the flesh is scraped out.

**COOK TIME:** 6 to 10 minutes; they will be soft like a cooked potato when done

**TO PREP:** Peel, cut in half, and scrape out the seeds. Cut into 1-inch cubes. Delicata and acorn squash do not need to be peeled.

## CORN ON THE COB

Corn holds sauce well, and it makes a great addition to a hot pot. You can also use canned baby corn, which is found in most grocery stores.

**COOK TIME:** 3 to 4 minutes

**TO PREP:** Cut the corn into ¾- to 1-inch-wide pieces.

## Dumplings, Fish Balls, and Meatballs

Asian markets usually have a plethora of frozen dumpling and meatball options. Fish balls are a lot of work to make, but the others are relatively easy to make at home.

### DUMPLINGS

Pre-made dumplings with myriad fillings add a great variety of flavors to hot pot. Or see pages 74–78 to make them from scratch.

**COOK TIME:** 5 to 7 minutes from frozen. Cooked dumplings float.

### FISH BALLS

Choose any variation, including ones stuffed with roe or another ground meat.

**COOK TIME:** 4 to 5 minutes from frozen. Cooked fish balls float.

### SHRIMP BALLS

Except for the pink flecks of color, these look like fish balls. Shrimp balls have a strong shrimp flavor, whereas fish balls tend to be much milder. See the Shrimp Paste Balls (page 79) recipe to make them from scratch.

**COOK TIME:** 5 to 6 minutes from frozen; 4 minutes for fresh. Cooked shrimp balls float.

### MEATBALLS

Made from a variety of meats like pork, beef, and lamb, Chinese meatballs are different from an Italian meatball, with a springy and more dense texture.

**COOK TIME:** 4 to 5 minutes from frozen; 2 minutes for fresh. Cooked meatballs float.

# FISH, MEAT, AND EGGS

· · · · · · · · · · · · · · · · · · · · ·

For many people, meat and seafood are the stars of the hot pot. Cook times are short because portions are traditionally very thinly cut. Thinly cut meats become opaque and change color when cooked through.

## *Thin-Sliced Meat*

Check out the frozen food section of an Asian grocery for pre-cut meats often labeled for hot pot or Korean barbecue. Many American groceries will have shaved beef available that was intended for Philly cheesesteaks that works well, too.

If you can't find them pre-sliced, here's how you can cut very thin slices of meat without any special equipment. You can do this for lamb, beef, pork, and poultry.

1.  To slice the meat, you'll need to freeze it partially, but not rock solid. Unwrap the meat; then place it, uncovered, on a tray or plate that fits in your freezer. Cut large pieces of meat into smaller pieces about 2 ½ to 3 inches wide so they freeze faster, and transfer to the freezer. For meat that is 1 inch at its thinnest dimension, it should be ready to slice after about 1 hour in the freezer. For a 2-inch cut, it should be ready in about 90 minutes, and for a 3-inch cut, check it at about 2 hours.

2. Once the meat is partially frozen, using your sharpest knife, slice against the grain of the meat. Cut as thinly as you can without the meat falling apart, usually $\frac{1}{16}$ to $\frac{1}{8}$ inch thick. The meat will squish if it is not frozen enough, and you'll have a hard time getting a good, clean slice. Put the meat back in the freezer for another 15 minutes and try again. If it's too hard to cut through, let it sit on the counter for 10 minutes and try again.

3. Fan out the slices like a deck of cards on a serving plate so that you can more easily grab an edge of one slice with tongs or chopsticks.

## Meats

For many, meats are the most important ingredient to a hot pot meal. Very thinly sliced meat works best because it cooks quickly. Asian grocery stores will often have thinly sliced meats in the freezer section that can be used for hot pot. Here are some of the best cuts for meat.

### LAMB

**BEST CUTS:** Shoulder and leg
**COOK TIME:** 15 to 20 seconds

### BEEF

Any cut of beef can be used with hot pot. If you'd like to eat it as a steak, you'll like it thinly sliced in your hot pot.
**BEST CUTS:** Brisket, short rib, or rib-eye steak
**COOK TIME:** 15 to 20 seconds

### BEEF TONGUE

Beef tongue has a rich, beefy flavor. The back of the tongue, or "neck side," is very tender and heavily marbled. The tip of the tongue has little to no marbling, and it is a chewier cut.
**COOK TIME:** 1 minute
**TO PREP:** Remove the skin and any connective tissue. Slice beef tongue thinly like regular cuts.

## PORK

**BEST CUTS:** Loin or belly. Thick-cut bacon will do if you can't find pork belly.
**COOK TIME:** 15 to 20 seconds

## POULTRY

**BEST CUTS:** Boneless, skinless chicken thighs and breast or boneless duck breast
**COOK TIME:** 15 to 20 seconds

## CHICKEN AND DUCK EGGS

**COOK TIME:** 5 to 6 minutes (soft-boiled); 10 to 12 minutes (hard-boiled); 3 to 5 minutes (poached, shorter time for a runny yolk)

## QUAIL EGGS

**COOK TIME:** 2 minutes (soft, for a runny yolk) to 4 minutes (hard-boiled)

## TRIPE AND INTESTINE

Choose pre-packaged versions in an Asian grocery store.
**COOK TIME:** 5+ minutes. Tripe really can't be overcooked. The longer it cooks, the more flavor it absorbs from the broth.
**TO PREP:** If it's not cleaned and parboiled, you will need to wash it thoroughly and then parboil and trim off any fat before slicing. You won't need to freeze it first.

## LIVER AND KIDNEY

**COOK TIME:** 1 minute
**TO PREP:** Slice thinly like regular cuts or thicker and then crosshatch.

# Fish and Shellfish

In general, any fish you enjoy will work for hot pot. Bigger fish that yield thicker fillets or even steaks hold together better. Smaller fish and thinner fillets may flake apart when cooked in the broth.

## FISH

**COOK TIME:** 30 to 60 seconds, depending on the thickness. Fish will become firm and opaque when cooked.
**TO PREP:** Remove any bones. For thick fillets or steaks, cube or slice on the bias into ¼-inch-thick pieces. For thin fillets, slice across the fillet into pieces about 1½ inches wide.

## SHELLFISH

Any shellfish you enjoy will work for hot pot. Scallops are great and require no prep. For shellfish in their shells, I recommend fresh clams or mussels. They should be alive before they are cooked.

**COOK TIME:** 1 to 2 minutes. Discard shellfish that do not open when cooked.

**TO PREP:** Scrub well to remove any sand or grit. To debeard mussels, hold them in one hand, use a towel or pliers to make it easier to grab the beard, and quickly yank it toward the hinge. Pulling toward the open side may kill the mussel. Soak clams and mussels in water for 20 minutes just before serving to allow them to expel sand and grit from inside the shell. Discard broken or cracked shells.

## SHRIMP

Buy shell-on, uncooked frozen shrimp in the freezer case. In most parts of the United States, almost all shrimp were frozen at some point. If buying unfrozen, confirm that it is truly fresh.

**COOK TIME:** 1 to 2 minutes, or until firm, opaque, and white and orange in color.

**TO PREP:** Defrost in the refrigerator for 12 hours. If the shrimp have not been deveined, carefully slice through the shell and into the meat lengthwise and devein.

You can leave the shell on or remove it. If removing, use the shells to make Fujian Seafood Broth (page 56).

## SQUID

Use your strainer to cook squid in the hot pot so that you don't lose it. Overcooked squid is tough and rubbery.

**COOK TIME:** 2 to 3 minutes

**TO PREP:** Frozen, pre-cut squid can be cooked from frozen. For fresh, cleaned squid, cut the body into rings or cut along one side to flatten it. Crosshatch the squid, and then cut into squares.

## CRAB OR LOBSTER

These are best purchased live the day of your hot pot or pre-cooked and frozen.

**COOK TIME:** 1 to 2 minutes (pre-cooked and thawed)

**TO PREP:** Crab and lobster can be cooked from frozen, but for lobster tails, defrost in the refrigerator for 10 to 12 hours so that the meat doesn't overcook. For fresh crabs, steam them in advance. Small crabs will cook in 5 to 6 minutes, and for large crabs and lobsters, allow 9 to 12 minutes. Separate the meaty legs, claws, and lobster tail for the hot pot. Reserve the rest of the carcass for making Fujian Seafood Broth (page 56).

# How Much Should I Buy?

It can be tricky to determine how much of any ingredient to have on hand or at the table for a hot pot meal. There is no one right formula, but here are some general guidelines to help you have enough food without having leftovers for a week.

**MEAT, SEAFOOD, AND TOFU:** ¾ pound (12 ounces) per person

**VEGETABLES AND MUSHROOMS:** ⅓ pound (about 5 ounces) per person

**DUMPLINGS, MEATBALLS, FISH BALLS, AND EGGS:** a combination of 4 to 6 total per person

**NOODLES:** ¼ pound (4 ounces) fresh noodles per person or 1 ½ ounces dried noodles per person

All of these amounts are totals for each ingredient group, so that means ¾ pound of a combination of meats, seafood, and tofu plus ⅓ pound of vegetables and so on would feed one person. For any group of diners, it's probable that for any person who doesn't eat seafood, another does not eat red meat, so it usually averages out fine. Do make sure to confirm allergies and eliminate any allergens. It is not worth the risk of cross-contamination even if you use separate hot pots.

# Leftovers?

The best part of the uncooked leftover ingredients is that they are already cut up and ready for stir-fry. Seafood is easily incorporated into seafood chowder along with remaining corn and potatoes. I'll admit that I usually discard most of the leftover broth from the hot pot even though I know it's got a lot of flavor. I freeze the unused broth that never made it to the hot pot for another meal.

# ABOUT THE RECIPES

In the following chapters, you'll find recipes to prepare your hot pot. Chapter 3 will focus on the broth, and chapter 4 will help you with dipping sauces and to make ingredients like noodles or shrimp balls from scratch. Chapters 5 and 6 put everything together with 19 hot pot recipes, each with a perfect combination of broth, sauces, and ingredients.

If you feel overwhelmed, start with a store-bought hot pot broth mix or even simply canned chicken broth. One of the best-known hot pot restaurant chains, Haidilao, includes plain water as an option on its hot pot menu. Remember, there is no right or wrong way to mix and match ingredients and broth. Sauces should taste good to you even if your friends and family wrinkle their noses at your combination of flavors. Once you get the hang of it, you can use these recipes as a launching point to create your own hot pot meals.

Don't let food allergies or dietary needs deter you from enjoying hot pot. Leave out troublesome ingredients or use the substitution tips in the recipes to make them your own.

*Sichuan Red Ma La Broth, page 38*

# CHAPTER THREE

## *Broths*

# SICHUAN RED MA LA BROTH

*Prep Time:* **45 MINUTES** *Cook Time:* **1 HOUR 30 MINUTES** *Makes* **10 CUPS**

This is the most popular hot pot broth in China, originating in the central province of Sichuan. Famous for its iconic red color, this popular broth has a fiery spiciness and unique mouth-numbing quality known as Ma La (málà, 麻辣). Pair this with a non-spicy broth like the Mandarin Duck Clear Broth (page 39) to balance out the heat.

1 to 3 cups whole dried red Sichuan chiles

4 tablespoons red Sichuan peppercorns

2 bay leaves

1 tablespoon Chinese five-spice powder

2 cups neutral oil (vegetable, canola, safflower, etc.)

½ cup minced scallions, both white and green parts

3 tablespoons peeled minced fresh ginger

6 garlic cloves, finely chopped

6 tablespoons Sichuan chili flakes

¼ cup fermented black beans (dòuchǐ, 豆豉)

5 tablespoons Sichuan broad bean chili paste

10 cups beef stock

½ cup Shaoxing wine

2 black cardamom pods

2 tablespoons sugar

1 teaspoon salt or low-sodium salt substitute like Ac'cent

1. In a medium bowl, soak the dried chiles in boiling water for at least 30 minutes.

2. In a spice grinder, grind the peppercorns and bay leaves to form a medium-ground powder. Transfer the ground spices to a small bowl and add the five-spice powder and just enough water to cover the spices. Let rest for 15 minutes.

3. Meanwhile, in a stockpot, heat the oil over low heat. Add the scallions, ginger, and garlic and cook for 6 to 8 minutes. Avoid browning the garlic.

4. Drain the whole chiles from step 1 and transfer to a cutting board. Remove any stems from the chiles; then mince the chiles to a paste-like texture.

5. Add the minced chiles, chili flakes, fermented black beans, and chili paste to the stockpot. Stir to combine and cook for 2 minutes, until fragrant.

6. Add the stock, ground spices (and soaking liquid) from step 2, wine, cardamom pods, sugar, and salt. Cover and bring to a boil. Reduce the heat to low and simmer for 10 minutes. Turn off the heat and let rest for at least 45 minutes.

# MANDARIN DUCK CLEAR BROTH

*Prep Time:* **15 MINUTES** *Cook Time:* **1 HOUR 15 MINUTES** *Makes* **10 CUPS** *Vegan*

Contrary to its name, there is no duck in this broth—it's vegan. Mandarin ducks (yuān yāng, 鸳鸯) mate for life, so they are associated with a well-matched pair. A "Mandarin Duck Pot" refers to a split hot pot, with a spicy Sichuan-style broth on one side and this mild broth on the other for the perfect pairing.

5 dried shiitake mushrooms

2 tablespoons neutral oil (vegetable, canola, safflower, etc.)

5 garlic cloves, finely chopped

6 scallions, both white and green parts, separated

5 (¼-inch-thick) slices peeled fresh ginger, smashed

10 cups water

8 dried Chinese red dates

1 tablespoon dried goji berries

1 tablespoon sugar

2 teaspoons salt or Ac'cent

1. In a small bowl, cover the mushrooms with boiling water. Cover and set aside.

2. In a stockpot, heat the oil over low heat until it shimmers. Add the garlic, white part of the scallions, and ginger and cook for 3 minutes. Stir occasionally to ensure the garlic doesn't brown.

3. Strain the mushrooms, reserving the soaking liquid, and transfer to a cutting board. Trim the woody stems.

4. Add the mushrooms, mushroom soaking liquid, water, and dates to the stockpot. Cover and bring to a boil; then reduce the heat to low and simmer for 1 hour.

5. Strain the broth, discarding the solids. Transfer the broth to the hot pot.

6. Cut the green part of scallions into 1-inch pieces; then add to the broth along with the goji berries, sugar, and salt just before serving.

PREP TIP: The simplest way to peel ginger is with a spoon. Hold the spoon like a paring knife and scrape off the skin.

# SICHUAN GREEN MA LA BROTH

*Prep Time:* **15 MINUTES** *Cook Time:* **1 HOUR 15 MINUTES** *Makes* **10 CUPS** *Vegan*

This variation on the Sichuan-style broth provides a different take on Ma La and has a cleaner and lighter flavor because it doesn't call for fermented black beans and warming spices like anise and cloves. Green Sichuan peppercorns are not unripe red Sichuan peppercorns but an entirely different variety with a more pronounced numbing flavor. Use more or fewer Thai chiles to adjust the spiciness.

4 tablespoons green Sichuan peppercorns

2 bay leaves

1 teaspoon fennel seeds

¼ cup neutral oil (vegetable, canola, safflower, etc.)

¼ cup pickled ginger, julienned

4 scallions, both white and green parts, cut into 1-inch pieces and separated

2 tablespoons Sichuan broad bean chili paste

3 garlic cloves, finely chopped

7 ounces Sichuan pickled vegetable (zhàcài, 榨菜) or kimchi

10 fresh green Thai chiles, trimmed

10 cups water

½ cup Shaoxing wine

Salt

1. In a spice grinder or blender, grind the peppercorns, bay leaves, and fennel seeds to a medium-ground powder. In a small bowl, place the spices with just enough water to cover. Let rest for at least 15 minutes.

2. In a stockpot, heat the oil over medium heat until it shimmers. Add the pickled ginger, white parts of the scallion, chili paste, and garlic. Fry for 2 minutes, stirring occasionally, until the garlic is softened.

3. Add the pickled vegetable and chiles and fry for 1 minute, or until fragrant.

4. Add the water and spice mixture, cover, and bring to a boil over high heat. When boiling, reduce the heat to low and simmer for 1 hour.

5. Remove from heat and add the wine. Season with salt to taste.

SUBSTITUTION TIP: If you want a richer broth, use a vegan broth instead of water.

# SICHUAN SPICY TOMATO BROTH

*Prep Time:* **30 MINUTES** *Cook Time:* **1 HOUR 15 MINUTES** *Makes* **10 CUPS** *Vegan*

This is a Sichuan-inspired variation of a classic tomato broth that incorporates Ma La flavors. This may not pack the same punch as the Red or Green Ma La broths, but combined with the tang of the tomatoes, this broth brings heat, numbing, sour, and umami all in one.

½ cup whole dried red Sichuan chiles

2 tablespoons red or green Sichuan peppercorns

1 tablespoon Chinese five-spice powder

¼ cup neutral oil (vegetable, canola, safflower, etc.)

1 tablespoon peeled, coarsely chopped fresh ginger

2 garlic cloves, coarsely chopped

2 tablespoons Sichuan chili flakes

2 tablespoons tomato paste

1 tablespoon Sichuan broad bean chili paste

1 (14.5-ounce) can diced tomatoes

8 cups water

¼ cup Shaoxing wine

1 tablespoon sugar

1 teaspoon salt or Ac'cent

1. Place the dried chiles in a small bowl. Add enough boiling water to cover. Cover the bowl and let rest for at least 30 minutes.

2. In a spice grinder or blender, grind the peppercorns to a medium-ground powder. Place in a small bowl with the five-spice powder and add just enough water to cover. Let rest for at least 15 minutes.

3. Meanwhile, in a stockpot, heat the oil over low heat. Add the ginger and garlic and cook for about 5 minutes, or until fragrant.

4. Drain the whole chiles from step 1 and transfer to a cutting board. Remove any stems from the chiles; then mince the chiles to a paste-like texture.

5. Add the minced chiles, chili flakes, tomato paste, and chili paste to the stockpot. Cook for 2 minutes.

6. Add the tomatoes with their juices, water, spice mixture (including the soaking liquid), wine, sugar, and salt. Stir to combine, cover, and bring the stock to a boil over high heat; then immediately reduce the heat to low. Simmer for 30 minutes.

# GUIZHOU SOUR FISH BROTH

*Prep Time:* **25 MINUTES** *Cook Time:* **1 HOUR** *Makes* **10 CUPS**

During my first trip to China, I visited Guiyang, the capital of the Guizhou province in southwest China near Sichuan province. Guizhou cuisine is often very spicy like neighboring Sichuan's cuisine. This broth uses pickled sour mustard in place of a hard-to-find Guizhou pickled chile (zāo làjiāo, 糟辣椒) and as a result is only mildly spicy. This also traditionally features local freshwater grass carp, but you can use any mild white fish.

1 egg white, beaten

1½ tablespoons Shaoxing wine

1 tablespoon cornstarch

1 teaspoon salt

1½ pounds catfish or any mild white fish fillets, skin on, scales removed

8 to 12 ounces pickled sour mustard

2 tablespoons neutral oil (vegetable, canola, safflower, etc.)

2 garlic chives or scallions, cut into 1-inch pieces

4 (¼-inch-thick) slices peeled fresh ginger, smashed

1 tablespoon Sichuan broad bean chili paste

8 cups chicken broth or water

1 teaspoon sugar

1 tomato, cut into wedges

1. In a large bowl, mix the egg white, wine, cornstarch, and salt. Stir to combine until the starch and salt are dissolved.

2. With the fish skin-side up, cut the fish on the bias at about a 30-degree angle relative to the cutting board into ⅜-inch-thick pieces. Add the fish pieces to the egg white mixture, stir gently to coat, and set aside to marinate.

3. Strain the pickled mustard, reserving the juice, and transfer to a cutting board and coarsely chop.

4. In a stockpot, heat the oil over medium-high heat. Add the pickled sour mustard, garlic chives, ginger, and chili paste and fry for 2 minutes, stirring to combine.

5. Add the broth, reserved pickling juice, and sugar. Cover and bring to a boil over high heat; then reduce the heat to low. Simmer for 15 minutes.

6. Strain the broth into the hot pot, discarding the solids. Add the marinated fish and tomato to the hot broth. Stir gently to separate the fish pieces, cover, and allow the residual heat to cook the fish for at least 10 minutes.

7. To begin your hot pot meal, carefully transfer the cooked fish to a serving dish. Turn on the hot pot and return the broth to a boil. Enjoy the cooked fish while you wait for the broth to get hot enough to cook other ingredients.

SUBSTITUTION TIP: Chinese pickled sour mustard (suāncài, 酸菜) is also sometimes labeled C'ai Chua. If you can't find it, use fermented sauerkraut instead.

PREP TIP: If making the broth in advance, keep the fish marinating in the refrigerator and pause the process at step 5. When ready to resume at step 6, bring the broth back to a boil, take the fish out of the refrigerator, and allow it to begin to warm up. When the broth boils, turn off the heat, add the fish, and cover. Allow the fish to cook for at least 10 minutes in the hot broth with the hot pot turned off.

# GUIZHOU PICKLED GREENS AND BEAN BROTH

*Prep Time:* **15 MINUTES, PLUS OVERNIGHT TO PRE-SOAK** *Cook Time:* **3 HOURS**
*Makes* **10 CUPS** *Vegan*

This broth is inspired by another Guizhou-style hot pot base, but I've swapped out the original pork broth for a vegetable broth. The dominant flavor comes from the pickled greens, providing a pleasant sourness, so a meat-based broth isn't essential to enjoying this tangy broth.

½ cup dried lima beans

1 teaspoon salt, divided

4 cups water

1 cup pickled sour mustard

1 tablespoon neutral oil (vegetable, canola, safflower, etc.)

3 large garlic cloves, minced

2 tablespoons peeled minced fresh ginger

1½ teaspoons (about 1 cube) red fermented bean curd

5 cups low-sodium vegetable broth

1 ear corn, cut into 1-inch pieces

1 tomato, cut into wedges

2 garlic chives, cut into 1-inch pieces

1.  In a medium bowl, combine the beans, ½ teaspoon of salt, and enough water to cover the beans by about 2 inches. Let soak overnight or at least 8 hours.

2.  In a medium pot, place the remaining ½ teaspoon of salt and the water. Bring to a boil over high heat. Drain the beans and add to the boiling water. Cover, reduce the heat to low, and simmer for 2 hours, or until the beans are soft.

3.  Strain the beans, reserving the cooking liquid. Set aside half of the beans, and in a small bowl, mash the other half with a fork or potato masher.

4.  Strain the pickled sour mustard, reserving the pickling juice, and transfer to a cutting board. Coarsely chop the mustard and set aside.

5. In a wok or large saucepan, heat the oil over medium heat until it shimmers. Add the garlic and ginger. Cook for about 1 minute; then add the fermented bean curd, stirring to break up the bean curd. Cook for another 30 seconds.

6. Add the pickled mustard to the wok and cook for 1 minute. Stir in the mashed beans and cook for about 1 minute. Remove from heat and set aside.

7. In a stockpot, combine 3 cups of reserved bean cooking liquid, the vegetable broth, and reserved pickling juice. Cover and bring to a boil over high heat.

8. Add the cooked beans, mashed beans, and mustard mixture to the stockpot. Cover and reduce the heat to low. Simmer for 30 minutes.

9. Transfer the broth to the hot pot and add the corn, tomato, and garlic chives. When ready to begin the hot pot meal, set the heat to high to bring to a boil.

PREP TIP: If using a vegetable broth concentrate or bouillon powder for the 5 cups of broth in step 7, follow the package instructions to mix 4 cups of broth, and then dilute with a fifth cup of water. Add this diluted broth and the other liquids to the stockpot. Test the broth, and if it needs more salt, add some or use more concentrate or bouillon powder to taste.

# YUNNAN MUSHROOM BROTH

*Prep Time:* **15 MINUTES**  *Cook Time:* **2 HOURS 15 MINUTES**  *Makes* **10 CUPS**  *Vegan*

Yunnan province is in the southwestern corner of China on the eastern tip of the Himalayan mountains. In the foothills of these mountains, foragers have found over 800 edible varieties of mushroom—most of them unique to the region. Local hot pot broths usually feature mushrooms found only in Yunnan. This recipe is an homage to the Yunnan broth using mushrooms that are easy to find.

10 cups water

1 teaspoon red Sichuan peppercorns

2 black cardamom pods

4 (¼-inch-thick) slices peeled fresh ginger, smashed

4 scallions, both green and white parts, divided

2 ounces dried mushrooms like shiitake, porcini, morels, or chanterelles, divided

Salt

2 teaspoons dried goji berries

8 to 10 dried red Chinese dates

1. In a large stockpot, combine the water, peppercorns, cardamom pods, ginger, and 2 scallions. Cover and bring to a boil over high heat; then reduce the heat to the lowest setting and simmer for 40 minutes.

2. When boiling, combine 2 cups of hot water from the stockpot with 1 ounce of dried mushrooms in a medium bowl. Cover and rehydrate the mushrooms for 30 minutes.

3. In a spice grinder or blender, grind the remaining 1 ounce of dried mushrooms to a powder. Set aside.

4. When the mushrooms have rehydrated, strain the mushrooms, reserving the soaking liquid, and transfer to a cutting board. Trim off the woody stems, return the mushrooms to the soaking liquid, and set aside.

5. Strain the stock, discarding the solids; then return the stock to the stockpot. Add the powdered mushrooms, rehydrated mushrooms, and reserved soaking liquid. Cover and simmer over low heat for 10 minutes. Season with salt.

6. Slice the remaining 2 scallions into 2-inch pieces. Add the scallions, goji berries, and dates to the broth when ready to start the hot pot. Wait to add these if making the broth well in advance.

SUBSTITUTION TIP: You can use a mushroom bouillon base instead of grinding dried mushrooms to a powder, but be aware that most mushroom bouillons are mostly salt or MSG. Better Than Bouillon's Mushroom Base is mostly mushroom but includes whey powder, so it is not vegan, only vegetarian.

# HUNAN CURED MEAT BROTH

*Prep Time:* **15 MINUTES** *Cook Time:* **1 HOUR 15 MINUTES** *Makes* **10 CUPS**

This Hunan-inspired broth uses cured meats as a base for its broth, but unfortunately, Hunan cured meats are not commonly exported. This recipe re-creates the flavors of this broth using cured meats that are easier to find, like Italian pancetta, bacon, and lap cheong sausage (which is made in the United States).

2 slices thick-cut bacon, diced

4 Chinese lap cheong sausage links, cut into ¼-inch-thick pieces

4 ounces pancetta, diced into ¼-inch cubes

3 (¼-inch-thick) slices peeled fresh ginger, smashed

3 garlic cloves, smashed

10 cups water

2 large pieces dried citrus peel

4 scallions, both white and green parts, cut into 1-inch pieces, divided

1 large daikon radish (about 1½ pounds), peeled and cut into 1-inch cubes

1. In a stockpot, cook the bacon over medium heat for about 5 minutes to render the fat. Add the lap cheong sausage and pancetta and cook for another 2 minutes to allow some of their fat to render in the pot.

2. Add the ginger and garlic and cook for 1 minute; then add the water, dried citrus peel, and white parts of the scallion. Cover and bring the broth to a boil over high heat; then reduce the heat to low. Simmer for 20 minutes.

3. Add the daikon radish to the stockpot. Cover and simmer for another 20 minutes.

4. Transfer the cooked radish to the hot pot.

5. Strain the broth, discarding the meats and aromatics, and add to the hot pot.

6. Top with the scallion greens before serving.

# MANDARIN LAMB BROTH

*Prep Time:* **20 MINUTES** *Cook Time:* **1 HOUR 35 MINUTES** *Makes* **10 CUPS**

In northern China, lamb is central to the hot pot experience, and this mild broth really brings out the flavor of the lamb. This method for making stock from raw bones can be used with beef, pork, or poultry bones as well.

1 pound raw lamb bones

12 cups water

1 tablespoon neutral oil (vegetable, canola, safflower, etc.)

4 (¼-inch-thick) slices peeled fresh ginger, smashed

2 scallions, both white and green parts, trimmed and halved

1 teaspoon salt

1 teaspoon ground white pepper

2 tablespoons dried goji berries

1. In a large bowl, soak the lamb bones in cold water for 30 minutes.

2. When the bones have been soaking for about 20 minutes, fill a large pot halfway with water and bring to a boil over high heat.

3. Drain the bones, transfer to the boiling water, and blanch for 2 minutes.

4. Drain the blanched bones using a colander. Rinse the bones under cold water for 20 to 30 seconds and then let drain completely. Set aside.

5. Rinse the pot and bring the water to a boil over high heat.

6. Meanwhile, in a separate large stockpot, heat the oil over medium heat until it shimmers. Transfer the rinsed lamb bones to the stockpot. Cook the bones for about 5 minutes, turning occasionally, until browned on all sides.

7. Add the ginger and scallions to the stockpot and carefully pour in the boiled water. Cover and simmer over low heat for 1 hour.

8. Strain the broth, discarding the bones and aromatics.

9. Add the salt and white pepper; then transfer the broth to the hot pot. To serve, add the goji berries and turn on the hot pot.

# HEILONGJIANG CLEAR BROTH

*Prep Time:* **5 MINUTES** *Cook Time:* **25 MINUTES** *Makes* **10 CUPS**

Heilongjiang province is in the northeastern corner of China. Bordering Inner Mongolia and Russia, it is a crossroads of cultures. The most iconic landmark in its capital city of Harbin is a Byzantine-style Orthodox Church, St. Sophia Cathedral. This clear broth is very mild and allows the flavors of the cooked ingredients and dipping sauce to shine.

10 cups water

1 cup Chinese garlic chives, cut into 1-inch pieces

2 scallions, both white and green parts, cut into 1-inch pieces

2 (¼-inch-thick) slices peeled fresh ginger, smashed

¼ cup dried shrimp (xiāmi, 蝦米 or 虾米)

2 tablespoons dried goji berries

1. In the hot pot, combine the water, garlic chives, scallions, ginger, and shrimp.

2. Cover, set the heat to high, and bring to a boil. When it reaches a boil, reduce the heat to the lowest setting and simmer for 20 minutes.

3. Add the goji berries 5 minutes before you begin the hot pot meal.

# CANTONESE CONGEE BROTH

*Prep Time:* **15 MINUTES** *Cook Time:* **1 HOUR 15 MINUTES** *Makes* **10 CUPS** *Vegan*

Congee is Chinese comfort food. It is a simple rice porridge that takes on the flavors of whatever you add to it so that its flavor improves throughout your hot pot meal. Congee hot pot goes especially well with seafood.

| | | |
|---|---|---|
| ½ cup white rice<br>12 cups water | 2 (¼-inch-thick) slices peeled fresh ginger, smashed | 1 teaspoon salt |

1. In a large bowl, rinse the rice using cool tap water. Stir with your hand and then drain the water. Repeat two more times.

2. Transfer the rinsed rice, water, ginger, and salt to a stockpot. Bring to a boil over high heat; then reduce the heat to a simmer.

3. Stir frequently to ensure the rice doesn't stick to the bottom of the pot.

4. Partially cover the pot and simmer for 1 hour, stirring occasionally. Do not completely cover the pot or it will boil over.

SUBSTITUTION TIP: For a more savory congee, substitute some or all of the water with a basic meat or vegetable broth of your choice.

PREP TIP: If you wash and drain uncooked rice and then freeze it for at least 8 hours, the congee will cook in about half the time. Using cooked rice will save only about 10 minutes. If you are using cooked rice, use about 1½ cups and reduce the water by a cup.

# CANTONESE PORK BONE BROTH

*Prep Time:* **20 MINUTES** *Cook Time:* **1 HOUR 35 MINUTES** *Makes* **10 CUPS**

This Cantonese-style broth is very mild and allows the flavors of the food to come through, making it a good counterpoint to a hot and spicy Sichuan-style broth. Cantonese cuisine comes from the southeastern regions of China surrounding Hong Kong.

1 pound raw pork bones

12 cups water

2 tablespoons neutral oil (vegetable, canola, safflower, etc.)

2 (¼-inch-thick) slices peeled fresh ginger, smashed

6 scallions, white part only

2 tablespoons Shaoxing wine

1 teaspoon ground white pepper

1 large daikon radish (about 1½ pounds), peeled, cut into 1-inch cubes

Salt

1. In a large bowl, soak the pork bones in cold water for 30 minutes.

2. When the bones have been soaking for about 20 minutes, fill a large pot halfway with water and bring to boil.

3. Drain the bones, transfer to the boiling water, and blanch for 2 minutes.

4. Drain the blanched bones using a colander. Rinse under cold water for 20 to 30 seconds and then let drain completely. Set aside.

5. Rinse the pot and bring the water to a boil over high heat.

6. Meanwhile, in a stockpot, heat the oil over medium heat until it shimmers. Transfer the drained pork bones to the stockpot. Cook the bones for about 5 minutes, turning occasionally, until browned on all sides.

7. Add the ginger, scallions, wine, and white pepper to the stockpot and carefully pour in the boiling water. Cover and simmer over low heat for 30 minutes.

8. Add the daikon radish, cover, and let simmer over low heat for another 30 minutes. Transfer the cooked radish to the hot pot.

9. Strain the broth, discarding all solids and add to the hot pot. Season with salt.

# HAINAN CHICKEN-COCONUT BROTH

*Prep Time:* **25 MINUTES** *Cook Time:* **1 HOUR 15 MINUTES** *Makes* **8 CUPS**

This broth is inspired by the popular Hainan-style poached chicken dish. Hainan is a tropical island making up the southernmost point of China, and its cuisine shares flavors found in Vietnam and Thailand. See Resources (page 127) for how to carve a chicken Chinese-style.

1 (2 ½- to 3-pound) whole
   small roasting chicken

½ teaspoon salt

8 cups coconut water

2 cups unsweetened
   coconut flakes

4 (¼-inch-thick) slices peeled
   fresh ginger, smashed

2 scallions, both white and
   green parts, quartered

1. Remove the neck and giblets from the chicken. Set aside the neck for the broth. Discard the giblets unless using as a hot pot ingredient.

2. In a large bowl, soak the chicken in cold water for 5 minutes; then drain and pat dry with paper towels. Rub the salt all over the chicken and set aside.

3. In a stockpot, combine the coconut water, coconut flakes, ginger, scallions, and the chicken neck. Cover and bring to a boil over high heat.

4. When the coconut water mixture comes to a boil, rinse off the salt from the chicken; then lower it gently into the stockpot, breast-side up. Cover and return the broth to a boil.

5. When boiling, use tongs to lift and tip the chicken to drain the cavity of any trapped water; then lower the chicken back into the pot. Cover and return to a boil.

6. Once boiling, reduce the heat to low and simmer for 5 minutes; then turn off the heat and let the chicken cook in the residual heat for 50 minutes.

7. Fill a large bowl or cooking pot halfway with water and ice. Transfer the cooked chicken to the ice bath, cover, and let cool for at least 15 minutes. When cooled, chop the chicken into bite-size pieces to serve with the hot pot.

8. Strain the broth, discarding the solids. Transfer the broth to the hot pot.

# CHRYSANTHEMUM BLOSSOM BROTH

*Prep Time:* **20 MINUTES** *Cook Time:* **1 HOUR 30 MINUTES** *Makes* **10 CUPS**

Popular in the Zhejiang province, the chrysanthemum hot pot was popularized by the Empress Dowager Cixi of the Qing Dynasty. The chrysanthemum hot pot was part of her regimen to maintain beauty and ensure a long life. This simple broth lets the chrysanthemum aroma shine through.

12 cups water

1 (2½- to 3-pound) whole chicken

2 tablespoons neutral oil (vegetable, canola, safflower, etc.)

2 scallions, both white and green parts, cut into 1-inch julienne

4 (¼-inch-thick) slices peeled fresh ginger, smashed

2 tablespoons dried chrysanthemum flowers or 4 chrysanthemum tea bags

1 tablespoon dried goji berries

8 dried Chinese red dates

1. In a large covered pot, bring the water to a boil.

2. Remove the neck and giblets from the chicken. Set aside the neck for the broth. Discard the giblets unless using as a hot pot ingredient.

3. Debone the chicken and remove the skin. Place the bones, skin, and carcass in a large bowl, cover with cold water, and let soak for 20 minutes; then drain and set aside. Reserve the chicken meat for your hot pot meal.

4. In a large stockpot, heat the oil over medium heat until it shimmers. Add the scallions and ginger and cook, stirring occasionally, for 2 minutes.

5. Add the chicken bones, neck, and skin to the stockpot and cook for 3 minutes, turning occasionally.

6. Carefully transfer the boiling water to the stockpot, and boil for 1 hour.

7. Strain the broth, discarding the bones, skin, and aromatics, and transfer to the hot pot. Add the dried chrysanthemum flowers, goji berries, and dates. Cover and let steep for 10 minutes to allow the flowers to hydrate and infuse the broth with their flavor and aroma. If using tea bags, remove them before serving.

# ZHEJIANG DRUNKEN CHICKEN BROTH

*Prep Time:* **15 MINUTES** *Cook Time:* **1 HOUR 15 MINUTES** *Makes* **8 CUPS**

Drunken chicken is usually prepared as a braised chicken dish. Heavily seasoned with Shaoxing wine and traditional Chinese herbs, it is viewed as the perfect companion to a cold winter day. This variation yields more of the broth so that it can be used for hot pot.

8 cups water

1 (2½- to 6-ounce) package Chinese herbal soup mix

4 (¼-inch-thick) slices peeled fresh ginger, smashed

½ teaspoon salt

½ teaspoon sugar

1 tablespoon plus 2 cups Shaoxing wine, divided

2 bone-in, skin-on chicken breasts

2 tablespoons dried goji berries

8 dried Chinese red dates

1. In a stockpot, combine the water, soup mix, and ginger. Cover and bring to a boil over high heat; then reduce the heat to low. Simmer for 45 minutes.

2. While the broth simmers, in a medium bowl, mix the salt, sugar, and 1 tablespoon of wine. Add the chicken breasts and stir well to coat. Cover and marinate in the refrigerator.

3. When the broth has been simmering for 45 minutes, add the marinated chicken and 1 cup of wine. Cover and continue to simmer for 10 minutes.

4. Transfer the cooked chicken to a cutting board and let cool for 5 minutes before carving. Using a Chinese cleaver or sharp chef's knife, cut each breast into 1-inch-wide pieces. Set aside on a serving plate for the hot pot meal.

5. Strain the broth, discarding the herbs and ginger, and transfer to the hot pot. Add the goji berries, dates, and the remaining 1 cup of wine. Return to a boil before adding hot pot ingredients to it.

**INGREDIENT TIP:** Look for Chinese herbal soup mixes that include Solomon's seal, dried lily bulbs, *Angelica sinensis*, fox nut, codonopsis root, astragalus root, overlord flower, and/or dried licorice root.

# FUJIAN SEAFOOD BROTH

*Prep Time:* **40 MINUTES**  *Cook Time:* **1 HOUR 30 MINUTES**  *Makes* **10 CUPS**

My family's history traces back to King Wu of the Zhou Dynasty, 1046 CE. In the 16th century, my 18th-great-grandfather was sent by the emperor to oversee Fujian province. Most of the family stayed in a small mountain village, but my great-grandfather left and went to the coastal city of Fuzhou, where he eventually joined the navy. Fuzhou remains a major port in China where seafood is abundant. I live near the Maine coast and wanted to feature local lobster in this Fujian-cuisine inspired broth.

2 live Maine lobsters (1¼ to 1½ pound each)

1 pound shell-on shrimp, deveined

1 tablespoon neutral oil (vegetable, canola, safflower, etc.)

2 (¼-inch-thick) slices peeled fresh ginger, smashed

1 bay leaf

1 teaspoon fennel seeds

1 teaspoon whole black peppercorns

¼ cup Shaoxing wine

2 plum tomatoes, quartered

8 cups water

1. In a large pot, bring ½ inch of water to a boil. Remove the rubber bands from the claws and place the lobsters in the pot, cover, and steam for 10 to 12 minutes, or until the shells become bright orange and the antennas break off with the slightest tug.

2. Remove the shrimp shells and set aside for the broth. Set the shrimp aside for hot pot.

3. Transfer the lobsters to a large bowl to cool. When cool enough to handle, remove the tail, claw, and knuckle meat, reserving the shells, juice, and cooking liquid. Set aside the meats for hot pot. Discard the feathery gills and the sand sac behind the eyes.

4.  In a large stockpot, heat the oil over medium heat. Add the shrimp shells and ginger and cook for 1 minute, or until the color of the shells changes. Add the lobster shells, breaking up any large pieces. Cook for another 5 minutes, stirring occasionally.

5.  Add the reserved cooking liquid, reserved lobster juice, bay leaf, fennel seeds, peppercorns, wine, tomatoes, and water. Cover and bring to a boil. Reduce the heat to low and simmer for 45 minutes.

6.  Strain the broth, discarding all solids, and transfer to the hot pot.

SUBSTITUTION TIP: You can use any combination of lobster, shrimp, crab shells, fish heads, or fish bones.

INGREDIENT TIP: The lobster tail meat should be sliced no thicker than ¼ inch and on the bias so that it reheats quickly in the hot pot. Since it is already cooked, you don't want to overcook the lobster meat, as it becomes tough.

# XINJIANG DABANJI BROTH

*Prep Time:* **25 MINUTES** *Cook Time:* **1 HOUR 15 MINUTES** *Makes* **10 CUPS**

Xinjiang province is located in the northwestern corner of China, bordering Pakistan, Kyrgyzstan, Kazakhstan, and Mongolia. It is the home to the Uighur people, and its cuisine is influenced as much by China as by its central Asian neighbors. One of the signature dishes of the region is DaBanJi or "big plate chicken," a beer-braised chicken dish. I've used this as the inspiration for this broth.

½ cup dried whole dried red Sichuan chiles

8 cups water

1 tablespoon neutral oil (vegetable, canola, safflower, etc.)

2 scallions, both white and green parts, minced

2 tablespoons peeled minced fresh ginger

3 garlic cloves, minced

2 tablespoons dark soy sauce

1 tablespoon sugar

1 teaspoon salt

1½ to 2 pounds chicken wings and thighs

1 (12-ounce) can beer (Xinjiang Wusu or any amber or brown ale)

1 star anise

1 cinnamon stick

1 black cardamom

1 teaspoon coarsely ground black pepper

1. In a small bowl, cover the dried chiles with boiling water. Let soak for at least 30 minutes. Drain and set aside.

2. In a medium pot, bring the water to a boil over high heat.

3. Meanwhile, in a stockpot, heat the oil over medium-high heat until it shimmers. Add the scallions, ginger, and garlic and cook for 2 minutes, stirring occasionally. Reduce the heat if needed to prevent the garlic from browning.

4. In a small bowl, combine the soy sauce, sugar, and salt.

5. Add the chicken and soy sauce mixture to the stockpot. Stir together to coat. Cook for 5 minutes or until the chicken pieces have begun to brown, stirring occasionally.

6. Transfer the pre-soaked chiles to a cutting board and mince to a paste-like texture.

7. Add the minced chiles, beer, star anise, cinnamon, cardamom, and black pepper to the stockpot. Cover and bring to a boil; then reduce the heat to low and simmer for 5 minutes.

8. Pour the boiling water into the stockpot. Cover and simmer for another 45 minutes.

9. Carefully transfer the cooked chicken to a serving plate. Strain the broth, discarding the aromatics, and transfer to the hot pot.

PAIRING TIP: If you've purchased a six-pack of beer to make this broth, serve the other five with your meal. In fact, maybe you should buy a couple six-packs!

# SHEEP SCORPION BROTH

*Prep Time:* **15 MINUTES, PLUS 1 HOUR TO SOAK**  *Cook Time:* **3 HOURS 30 MINUTES**
*Makes* **10 CUPS**

You can taste the influence of central Asia and the Silk Road in the cumin that flavors this broth. As exciting as it would be to include scorpions in a broth, too, this classic recipe got its name from a sheep's vertebrae bone. The cross section of that bone is thought to resemble a scorpion. Sheep scorpion is a braised mutton dish that comes from Inner Mongolia, but it is popular across northern and western China. It is the inspiration for this hot pot broth.

2 pounds sheep neck and spine bones

12 cups water

2 tablespoons neutral oil (vegetable, canola, safflower, etc.)

5 whole dried red Sichuan chiles

4 scallions, both white and green parts, cut into 1-inch pieces

3 bay leaves

2 (¼-inch-thick) slices peeled fresh ginger, smashed

1 cinnamon stick

1 tablespoon cumin seeds

1 teaspoon fennel seeds

½ teaspoon whole cloves

2½ tablespoons dark soy sauce

2½ tablespoons Shaoxing wine

2 tablespoons soy sauce

1 teaspoon sugar

1. In a large bowl, soak the sheep bones in cool water for at least 1 hour.

2. In a large pot, add the water and bring to a boil over high heat.

3. Drain the bones and transfer to a stockpot. Fill with enough cool water to cover the bones. Cover and bring to a boil over high heat; then remove from heat. Drain the boiled bones, transfer to a large bowl, and set aside.

4. Rinse and dry the stockpot. In the clean stockpot, heat the oil over medium heat.

5. Add the chiles, scallions, bay leaves, ginger, cinnamon stick, cumin seeds, fennel seeds, and cloves. Cook for 2 minutes; then add the boiled sheep bones.

6. In a small bowl, mix the dark soy sauce, wine, soy sauce, and sugar, stirring to dissolve. Pour over the sheep bones.

7. Carefully transfer the boiling water to the stockpot. Cover and return the water to a boil; then reduce heat to low and simmer for 3 hours. Check the pot after 1 hour 30 minutes to make sure that the broth is still covering the bones. If not, add more water to cover.

8. After 3 hours, the meat should be fall-off-the-bone tender. Transfer the bones and broth to the hot pot to serve.

PREP TIP: Use a slotted spoon or kitchen tongs to transfer the sheep bones to the hot pot first; then you can more easily pour the broth. You can also strain the broth first to remove the spices if you prefer.

# TOMATO BROTH

*Prep Time:* **25 MINUTES** *Cook Time:* **1 HOUR** *Makes* **10 CUPS** *Vegan*

Tomatoes first came to China in the late 16th century, about the same time that they were introduced to Italy. Tomatoes have not become as central to the cuisine as they have in Italy, but in hot pot, one of the most ubiquitous styles of broth is the tomato broth. Interestingly, China is the world's largest producer of tomatoes, accounting for over 31 percent of the world's tomatoes.

2 tablespoons neutral oil (vegetable, canola, safflower, etc.)

2 shallots, diced

2 garlic cloves, minced

2 tablespoons tomato paste

1 tablespoon sugar

5 plum tomatoes, cut into wedges, divided

1 pint cherry tomatoes, halved

8 cups water

1 teaspoon salt

1 teaspoon ground white pepper

1. In a stockpot, heat the oil over low heat. Add the shallots and garlic and sauté for 8 minutes, until the shallots are translucent.

2. Add the tomato paste and sugar, stirring to break up the paste, and cook for another 2 minutes, or until everything is fully incorporated.

3. Add half of the tomato wedges and all of the cherry tomatoes to the stockpot. Cook for another 10 minutes, or until the tomatoes have broken down. Stir occasionally and use a large spoon to break up and crush the tomatoes.

4. Add the water to the stockpot. Cover and bring to a boil; then reduce the heat to low and simmer for 30 minutes.

5. Add the remaining tomato wedges, salt, and white pepper and transfer to the hot pot to serve.

SUBSTITUTION TIP: You can substitute 1 (14-ounce) can of diced tomatoes for the fresh plum and cherry tomatoes.

# BUDDHIST CLEAR BROTH

*Prep Time:* **10 MINUTES**  *Cook Time:* **40 MINUTES**  *Makes* **10 CUPS**  *Vegan*

Buddhism has influenced Chinese culture for centuries. There are a couple of food prohibitions in Buddhism including alcohol and certain pungent "spices" like onion, garlic, shallots, chives, and leeks. These foods, all members of the allium family, are said to create anger and passion. While not all Buddhists adhere to this prohibition, I've assembled a vegan broth that steers clear of these foods.

8 cups water

1 (2½- to 6-ounce) package Chinese herbal soup mix

1 small daikon radish, peeled and cut into 1-inch cubes

1 ear corn, cut into 1-inch pieces

1½ teaspoons red fermented bean curd

3 (¼-inch-thick) slices peeled fresh ginger, smashed

2 pieces dried citrus peel

1 tablespoon soy sauce

2 tablespoons dried goji berries

1 teaspoon toasted sesame oil

8 dried Chinese red dates

1. In the hot pot, combine the water, herbal soup mix, daikon radish, corn, fermented bean curd, ginger, citrus peel, and soy sauce. Cover and bring to a boil over high heat; then reduce the heat to low and simmer for 30 minutes.

2. Add the goji berries, sesame oil, and dates 5 minutes before you begin your hot pot meal.

INGREDIENT TIP: When shopping for Chinese herbal soup mix packets, look for combinations that include Solomon's seal, dried lily bulbs, *Angelica sinensis*, fox nut, codonopsis root, astragalus root, overlord flower, and/or dried licorice root.

*Handmade Lo Mein Noodles, page 80*

# CHAPTER FOUR

# Sauces and Ingredients

# SETTING UP YOUR SAUCE BAR

The sauce bar is essential to any hot pot meal because it allows you to personalize your eating experience. You don't have to have every item on this list, but the key is to provide enough variety so guests can invent their dipping sauce.

## PRE-MADE SAUCES

Cilantro-Sesame Oil (page 69)

Ginger-Scallion Oil (page 70)

Hoisin sauce

Oyster sauce

Sa cha barbecue sauce
  (shā chá jiàng, 沙茶酱)

Sesame Sauce (page 68)

Sichuan Chili Oil
  (page 71) or chili oil

Soy sauce

Toasted sesame oil

XO sauce

## VINEGARS

Chinese black vinegar

Rice wine vinegar

## MINCED INGREDIENTS

Cilantro

Garlic

Ginger

## DRY SPICES

Chili powder/flakes

Salt

Sugar

Toasted sesame seeds

## OTHER

Red fermented bean curd
  (hóng fǔrǔ, 紅腐乳)

1. Select an open space on your counter or sideboard to set up your sauce bar. Set out the ingredients you've selected like a salad bar, along with the bowls needed to mix the sauces. Include more bowls than the number of diners since some people will want to make multiple sauces.

2. For pre-made sauces, vinegars, wines, and fermented bean curd, leave them in their original containers. If you've made sesame sauce and/or Sichuan chili oil, set out a bowl of each. Plan on a cup of sesame sauce for every 3 to 4 diners and about a cup of chili oil. For sauces that are not easily poured, include a dedicated spoon.

3. For minced ingredients, use the smallest bowls you have or ramekins. You'll want a tablespoon or two per diner of each ingredient, and include a dedicated spoon for each minced ingredient.

4. For dry spices, leave them in their store packaging if possible. Salt and sugar can be in ramekins, but make sure to clearly label them and include a dedicated spoon for each ramekin.

# SESAME SAUCE

*Prep Time:* **5 MINUTES** *Makes* **1¼ CUPS OR 5 SERVINGS** *Vegan*

Sesame sauce is one of the most common sauce bases in hot pot, especially in northern China. You can use it on its own and include it on the sauce bar for diners to use as the base of their personal creation. With a toasted, nutty flavor, it goes well with any broth and any ingredient.

½ cup Chinese sesame paste

½ cup water

3 tablespoons toasted sesame oil

1 cube (about 1 tablespoon) red fermented bean curd

2 teaspoons sugar

1½ teaspoons brown sugar

½ teaspoon salt

1. Stir the sesame paste thoroughly to re-incorporate any oil that has separated from the paste.

2. In a small bowl, combine the sesame paste, water, sesame oil, fermented bean curd, sugar, brown sugar, and salt. Use a whisk to combine into a smooth sauce.

**SUBSTITUTION TIP:** Chinese sesame paste is made from ground toasted sesame seeds, whereas tahini is made from ground raw sesame seeds. To replicate the flavor of Chinese sesame paste using tahini, combine ¼ cup plus 1 tablespoon of tahini with 3 tablespoons of toasted sesame oil to make the equivalent of ½ cup of Chinese sesame paste.

**INGREDIENT TIP:** When shopping for Chinese sesame paste, avoid the sesame-peanut version (zhīma huāshēngjiàng, 芝麻花生酱). It looks the same, but the taste is not. It is also usually poorly labeled "Sesame Paste," with no mention of the peanuts. To ensure that you are getting the right type of paste, look for only the Chinese characters (芝麻酱) on the label, and verify the ingredient list contains no peanuts, especially if you're allergic.

# CILANTRO-SESAME OIL

*Prep Time:* **10 MINUTES**  *Makes* **ABOUT 1½ CUPS OR 5 SERVINGS**

In central and south China, an oil-based sauce is more common. This combination is easy to create on the fly at your sauce bar. You can also easily prepare a batch in advance for your diners, but it's best made fresh not too far in advance. This goes especially well with hot and spicy broths, as it helps absorb some of the heat and cleanse the palate.

1 cup toasted sesame oil

½ cup minced cilantro

¼ cup minced garlic

¼ cup minced scallion

2½ cubes (about 2½ tablespoons) red fermented bean curd

2 tablespoons oyster sauce

1¼ teaspoons salt

In a medium bowl, combine the sesame oil, cilantro, garlic, scallion, fermented bean curd, oyster sauce, and salt. Stir to combine.

# GINGER-SCALLION OIL

*Prep Time:* **10 MINUTES** *Makes* **1¼ CUPS OR 5 SERVINGS** *Vegan*

Thanks to its clean, fresh taste, this oil is often used alone as a dumpling dipping sauce. It can also be combined with other sauces anytime you are looking to add ginger and scallion flavors.

2½ tablespoons peeled grated fresh ginger

5 scallions, both white and green parts, minced

2 teaspoons salt

1 teaspoon ground white pepper

1 cup neutral oil (vegetable, canola, safflower, etc.)

1. In a medium heat-proof bowl, combine the ginger, scallions, salt, and white pepper.

2. In a small saucepan, heat the oil over medium heat until it reaches about 250°F. If you do not have an instant-read thermometer, place a bamboo chopstick or skewer in the oil. When small bubbles begin to form from the chopstick, the temperature should be about 225 to 250°F.

3. Carefully pour the hot oil over the ingredients in the bowl; then stir to combine with a heat-proof utensil.

INGREDIENT TIP: You can make this ahead and store in a clean sealed glass jar. Make sure the oil is cooled before transferring it to the glass jar. Always use a clean utensil when using it, and it will keep in the refrigerator for up to a month.

# SICHUAN CHILI OIL

*Prep Time:* **10 MINUTES**   *Cook Time:* **30 MINUTES**   *Makes* **2½ CUPS**   *Vegan*

This versatile spicy chili oil is used in countless other classic Chinese recipes, and it adds some pizazz to most anything. Add it to your dipping sauce to introduce Sichuan Ma La flavors.

2 cups neutral oil (vegetable, canola, safflower, etc.)

4 tablespoons red Sichuan peppercorns

6 star anise

1 piece cinnamon stick

4 pieces dried galangal root

3 garlic cloves, crushed

2 shallots, halved

2 teaspoons whole cloves

2 bay leaves

2 pods black cardamom (optional)

1 cup Sichuan chili flakes

1 teaspoon salt

1. In a medium saucepan, combine the oil, peppercorns, star anise, cinnamon stick, galangal root, garlic, shallots, cloves, bay leaves, and cardamom (if using).

2. Heat the oil over medium heat for 2 minutes or until bubbles begin to form from the spices. Reduce the heat slightly and continue to let bubble, reducing the heat further if the garlic or shallots start to brown. Once the mixture is bubbling, allow the mixture to steep over low heat for at least 20 minutes, until the aromatics infuse the oil.

3. Meanwhile, in a large heat-proof bowl, place the Sichuan chili flakes.

4. Carefully strain the hot oil mixture through a fine-mesh metal strainer and into the bowl with the chili flakes. Discard the aromatics.

5. Stir in the salt with a heat-proof utensil. Let cool completely before serving.

SUBSTITUTION TIP: Increase or decrease the amount of chili flakes by as much as a ½ cup to change the spiciness of the finished oil.

# JEFF'S HOT AND SOUR DIPPING SAUCE

*Prep Time:* **5 MINUTES** *Makes* **ABOUT 1¼ CUPS OR 5 SERVINGS** *Vegan*

I've been making variations of this simple dipping sauce for hot pot and dumplings for as long as I can remember. You can use plain hot chili oil and rice wine vinegar, but Sichuan chili oil and Zhenjiang vinegar each bring an additional depth of flavor if you have them.

10 tablespoons Sichuan Chili Oil (page 71)

3 tablespoons plus 1 teaspoon Chinese Zhenjiang vinegar

5 teaspoons soy sauce

5 teaspoons toasted sesame oil

5 teaspoons minced scallion, both white and green parts

5 teaspoons minced garlic

In a small bowl, combine the chili oil, vinegar, soy sauce, sesame oil, scallion, and ginger. Stir to combine.

**SUBSTITUTION TIP:** If you don't have homemade Sichuan chili oil, you can use any number of store-bought chili oil options, such as basic Asian hot chili oil, a Lao Gan Ma brand chili oil, or another favorite of mine, Lee Kum Kee's Guizhou-Style Black Bean Chili Sauce.

# CHILE-LIME SAUCE

*Prep Time:* **5 MINUTES** *Makes* **ABOUT 1¼ CUPS OR 5 SERVINGS** *Vegan*

The combination of lime and chiles creates a flavor that is reminiscent of Thai and Vietnamese foods. It goes especially well with the Hainan Chicken–Coconut Broth (page 53).

¼ cup minced fresh chiles

¼ cup peeled minced fresh ginger

¼ cup minced garlic

¼ cup rice wine vinegar

¼ cup freshly squeezed lime juice (about 2 limes)

¼ cup minced fresh cilantro

5 teaspoons toasted sesame oil

5 teaspoons sugar

5 teaspoons water or broth

2 ½ teaspoons salt

In a small bowl, combine the chiles, ginger, garlic, vinegar, lime juice, cilantro, sesame oil, sugar, water, and salt and stir to dissolve the sugar and salt.

# MUSHROOM DUMPLINGS

*Prep Time:* **1 HOUR 30 MINUTES** *Cook Time:* **10 MINUTES** *Makes* **36 TO 48 DUMPLINGS** *Vegan*

This vegetable dumpling packs a flavorful and juicy punch without any meat, thanks to the mushroom filling. To create the juiciness, this recipe includes a few tablespoons of oil infused with ginger, scallions, and garlic. Together, they provide rich flavors that are just as satisfying as a meaty dumpling.

3 tablespoons neutral oil (vegetable, canola, safflower, etc.), divided

2 cups finely chopped mushrooms of choice (shiitake, portobello, oyster, etc.)

3 cups finely chopped Chinese cabbage

2 large carrots, grated

4 scallions, both green and white parts, minced

1 tablespoon peeled minced fresh ginger

1 garlic clove, minced

1 tablespoon soy sauce

1 tablespoon toasted sesame oil

½ teaspoon ground white pepper

1 (12- to 16-ounce) package round dumpling wrappers (or make your own; see page 81)

1. In a wok or large frying pan, heat 1 tablespoon of oil over high heat until it shimmers. Add the mushrooms and stir-fry until they release their liquid, about 2 minutes. Continue to cook until the liquid has evaporated, about 1 minute.

2. Add the cabbage and carrots and stir-fry for 2 minutes. Add the scallions, ginger, and garlic and stir-fry for another 30 seconds, or until all the liquid has evaporated. Remove from heat.

3. Transfer the filling mixture to a medium bowl and stir in the soy sauce, the remaining 2 tablespoons of oil, the sesame oil, and white pepper. Set aside on the counter and allow to cool completely.

4. Place a dumpling wrapper on a work surface or cutting board. Using your fingertip, moisten half the interior edge of a wrapper with water.

5. Place about a tablespoon of filling onto the center of a wrapper. Fold the edge over the filling to form a semicircle and press the edge to seal. Repeat with the remaining wrappers and filling.

INGREDIENT TIP: If using dried mushrooms, rehydrate them first in a bowl of hot water. Make sure to trim any woody stems from your mushrooms, whether fresh or dry.

# PORK AND SHRIMP DUMPLINGS

*Prep Time:* **45 MINUTES** *Cook Time:* **10 MINUTES** *Makes* **36 TO 48 DUMPLINGS**

Some of my earliest memories of cooking in the kitchen are folding dumplings as a child. These dumplings are great for boiling in your hot pot, but they can also be steamed or steam-fried on their own.

4 scallions, both white and green parts, minced

2 tablespoons peeled minced fresh ginger

¼ teaspoon Chinese five-spice powder

2 tablespoons neutral oil (vegetable, canola, safflower, etc.)

⅔ pound ground pork

⅓ pound shrimp, shelled and deveined, chopped

2 cups finely chopped Napa cabbage

1 tablespoon Shaoxing wine

1 tablespoon soy sauce

½ cup water

1 (12- to 16-ounce) package round dumpling wrappers (or make your own; see page 81)

1. **TO MAKE THE FILLING:** In a large heat-proof bowl, combine the scallions, ginger, and five-spice powder.

2. In a small saucepan, heat the oil. When the oil is hot enough, bubbles will form when you place the tip of a bamboo skewer or chopstick into the oil. Carefully pour the hot oil over the ingredients in the large bowl; then stir to combine.

3. Add the pork, shrimp, cabbage, wine, and soy sauce to the oil mixture and stir to combine. Stir the filling mixture vigorously in one direction for at least 2 minutes. The filling will get shiny and paste-like. This will help trap moisture as well as lead to a firmer texture when cooked.

4. Add the water; then stir for another 60 seconds or until the water is fully incorporated with no standing water.

5. **TO MAKE THE DUMPLINGS:** Place a dumpling wrapper on a work surface or a cutting board. Using your fingertip, moisten half of the interior edge of a wrapper with water.

6. Place about a tablespoon of filling onto the center of a wrapper. Fold the edge over the filling to form a semicircle and press the edge to seal. Repeat with the remaining wrappers and filling.

PREP TIP: Dumplings are easy to overfill. If you need a visual reference, 1 tablespoon of filling would be a ball about 1¼ inch in diameter.

# XINJIANG LAMB DUMPLINGS

*Prep Time:* **45 MINUTES** *Cook Time:* **10 MINUTES** *Makes* **36 TO 48 DUMPLINGS**

This recipe is inspired by dumplings from the western Xinjiang province where the Silk Road extended into central Asia. They include flavors from both East and West! Lamb has a stronger flavor than beef or pork, and when combined with cumin and black pepper, these dumplings are much richer than what you find in most American Chinese restaurants.

1 pound ground lamb

1 small red onion, finely chopped

2 tablespoons peeled minced fresh ginger

2 garlic cloves, minced

1 tablespoon ground cumin

1 teaspoon ground coriander

1 teaspoon freshly ground black pepper

½ cup water

1 tablespoon soy sauce

1 (12- to 16-ounce) package round dumpling wrappers (or make your own; see page 81)

1. **TO MAKE THE FILLING:** In a large bowl, combine the lamb, onion, ginger, garlic, cumin, coriander, and pepper. Stir the filling mixture vigorously in one direction for at least 2 minutes. The filling will get shiny and paste-like. This will help trap moisture as well as lead to a firmer texture when cooked.

2. Add the water and soy sauce and stir again in the same direction until the liquid is fully incorporated, or at least 60 seconds.

3. **TO MAKE THE DUMPLINGS:** Place a dumpling wrapper on a work surface. Using your fingertip, moisten half the interior edge of a wrapper with water.

4. Place about a tablespoon of filling onto the center of a wrapper. Fold the edge over the filling to form a semicircle and press the edge to seal. Repeat with the remaining wrappers and filling.

SUBSTITUTION TIP: You can use the same dough used for Handmade Lo Mein Noodles (page 80) to make wrappers for these dumplings. Dumplings made with homemade wrappers will have a more toothsome chew that is similar to most restaurant dumplings.

# SHRIMP PASTE BALLS

*Prep Time:* **15 MINUTES, PLUS 30 MINUTES TO CHILL** *Cook Time:* **5 MINUTES**
*Makes* **12 BALLS**

Shrimp balls are a very popular hot pot ingredient. Though they're generally only available at an Asian grocery, the good news is they are easy to make! I don't know why, but I sometimes think that shrimp balls have more shrimp flavor than actual shrimp.

8 ounces shrimp, shelled and deveined

1 teaspoon cornstarch

1 teaspoon Shaoxing wine

½ teaspoon salt

½ teaspoon ground white pepper

1. In a food processor, pulse the shrimp in 2-second bursts 6 to 8 times, or until the shrimp is very finely minced but retains some texture.

2. Transfer the minced shrimp to a medium bowl and add the cornstarch, wine, salt, and white pepper.

3. Using chopsticks, stir the shrimp mixture vigorously in one direction for 30 seconds; then give yourself a rest. Repeat the stirring process 15 times. The mixture will become shiny and more paste-like.

4. Cover the mixture and refrigerate for at least 30 minutes.

5. When ready for hot pot, use a pair of spoons to form 12 equal-size balls (about an inch in diameter) and lower them gently into the boiling hot pot broth. When they float, let them cook through for another minute, about 4 minutes total.

# HANDMADE LO MEIN NOODLES

*Prep Time:* **1 HOUR** *Cook Time:* **5 MINUTES** *Makes* **4 SERVINGS** *Vegan*

Making lo mein noodles from scratch is simpler than you may think! The only tools you need are a rolling pin and a knife. You can also use this dough (see tip) to make dumpling wrappers for Mushroom Dumplings (page 74), Pork and Shrimp Dumplings (page 76), or Xinjiang Lamb Dumplings (page 78).

| 2 cups bread flour, plus more for dusting | ½ cup water | ¼ teaspoon salt |

1.  In a large, wide bowl, combine the flour, water, and salt.

2.  Using chopsticks, stir the mixture until the water is absorbed. The dough will not be a cohesive ball but lots of small clumps. Using your hand, form the dough into a ball and knead it for 30 seconds. The dough will feel dry and stiff at this stage.

3.  Cover the dough with another bowl. Let the dough rest for 15 minutes; then knead it for 30 seconds. Cover again and let it rest for another 15 minutes. Knead it one last time for 30 seconds. Cover and let rest one final time for another 15 minutes. Do not skip the rest periods. It's okay if a rest period exceeds 15 minutes. At each stage, you will notice the dough becoming smoother and softer.

4.  To begin rolling out the dough, divide the dough in half. Place one half back in the bowl and cover while you work on the other half.

5.  Lightly dust a work surface and rolling pin with flour. Roll out the dough into a long rectangular shape until it is about ⅛ inch thick or less. Dust with more flour as needed. If the dough springs back, making it difficult to roll it thinly enough, cover with a clean dish towel, let the dough rest for 10 minutes to relax the gluten, and then resume rolling.

6. Dust generously with more flour. Fold the dough over once so the two long edges meet.

7. Cut into your desired noodle width, usually ⅛ to ½ inch wide. Slice rather than chop to avoid pressing down and sealing the noodle edges. Gently transfer the cut noodles to a plate and dust with more flour to prevent sticking. Cover with a clean dish towel until ready to use.

INGREDIENT TIP: To use this recipe to make dumpling wrappers for any of the recipes in this book, combine 3 cups of bread flour, ¾ cup of water, and ¼ teaspoon of salt to make enough dough for 36 dumplings. At step 4, use one-third of the dough and roll it with your hands into a thick rope. Divide this into quarters; then divide each of these into three equal pieces. Roll each piece into a ball; then press flat onto a work surface with the heel of your hand. Using a small rolling pin, roll into a 3-inch wrapper.

*Wild Mushroom Hot Pot, page 84*

# CHAPTER FIVE

# *Vegetable Hot Pots*

This chapter's recipes are more pairing suggestions than conventional recipes. The formal cooking happens when you make your broth and/or sides. A few reminders to share with your diners:

- Everyone can personalize their meal by cooking their choice of ingredients a couple of bites at a time.
- Cook a couple of ingredients at a time and avoid overcrowding the hot pot, as that slows cooking times for everyone. Don't cook your whole meal at once!
- Some ingredients take longer to cook, like taro root, so while they cook, cook something that takes less time, like tofu.
- Traditionally, noodles are cooked late in a meal when the broth has absorbed more flavors from cooking, but remember: The only rule of hot pot is that there are no hot pot rules!
- Refer to chapter 2 for ingredient prep and cooking times if needed and chapter 6 for more tips.

# WILD MUSHROOM HOT POT

*Prep Time:* **45 MINUTES** *Make-Ahead Time:* **2 HOURS 15 MINUTES**
*Makes* **4 SERVINGS** *Vegan*

You will be hard-pressed to find the same variety of wild mushrooms in your grocery store as foragers do in the mountains of the Yunnan province. However, more and more grocery stores are carrying a larger variety of cultivated mushrooms, like shiitake, enoki, shimeji, and king trumpet. Experiment with what you can find!

**MAKE IN ADVANCE**

1 batch Yunnan Mushroom Broth (page 46)

12 Mushroom Dumplings (page 74)

1 batch Cilantro-Sesame Oil (page 69)

Sichuan Chili Oil (page 71)

6 ounces dried mung bean (glass) noodles

1½ pounds fresh mushrooms of choice

8 ounces firm or extra-firm tofu, cut into 1-inch cubes

8 ounces dwarf bok choy, halved lengthwise

8 ounces choy sum, cut into 1-inch-wide pieces

1 medium peeled lotus root, cut into ½-inch-thick discs

1 medium delicata squash, halved, seeded, and cut into ½-inch-thick pieces

1. Prepare the broth, dumplings, cilantro-sesame oil, and chili oil according to instructions.

2. In a large bowl, soak the noodles in warm water for 15 minutes, or until pliable. Set aside.

3. Assemble the hot pot ingredients by placing the dumplings, mushrooms, tofu, bok choy, choy sum, lotus root, and squash on large plates and setting them on the table.

4.  Set up the hot pot at the table and bring the pre-cooked broth to a boil over high heat.

5.  Lay out the ingredients for the sauce bar, including the cilantro-sesame oil and chili oil, and set the table with chopsticks, strainers, and other utensils.

6.  When the broth comes to a boil, drain the noodles and transfer to a medium bowl to serve.

7.  Using chopsticks, a hot pot strainer, or tongs, lower your chosen ingredients into the hot broth. Once cooked through, remove from the broth and eat with your dipping sauces.

PAIRING TIP: A British or Irish stout's sweet, full-bodied flavor goes well with the earthy and savory flavors of mushrooms.

INGREDIENT TIP: To allow the tofu to absorb more broth and flavor, compress it using a weight to squeeze out its liquid before cutting into cubes. To press out even more water, freeze the tofu in its original packaging; then defrost and compress.

# PATH TO ENLIGHTENMENT HOT POT

*Prep Time:* **35 MINUTES** *Make-Ahead Time:* **1 HOUR 30 MINUTES, PLUS 8 HOURS TO PRE-SOAK** *Makes* **4 SERVINGS** *Vegan*

One Buddhist food tradition centers around the giving of food to hungry ghosts. The hungry ghost represents greed and attachment. By giving away something you crave, you release yourself from some of your greed and attachments. Try starting your hot pot meal by adding your favorite ingredient to the hot pot and giving it away to a hungry ghost or one of your fellow diners! Additionally, when preparing your dumplings, leave out the garlic and scallions if you wish to adhere to the Buddhist prohibition of the five pungent spices.

MAKE IN ADVANCE

1 batch Buddhist Clear Broth (page 63)

1 batch Sesame Sauce (page 68)

12 Mushroom Dumplings (page 74)

2 to 3 ounces dried bean curd stick

16 ounces fresh lo mein noodles

12 ounces fresh mushrooms (enoki, oyster, king trumpet, etc.)

8 ounces Chinese broccoli, cut into 1-inch pieces

8 ounces tatsoi, cut into 1-inch pieces

8 ounces spinach

6 ounces pressed tofu, cut into bite-size pieces

½ small acorn squash (about 8 to 12 ounces), seeded and cut into 1-inch cubes

1 medium peeled lotus root, cut into ½-inch-thick discs

1 medium sweet potato, cut into ½-inch-thick discs

1. Prepare the broth, sesame sauce, and dumplings according to instructions.

2. In a 9-by-13-inch casserole dish, soak the bean curd stick in cool water. Cover and allow to soak for at least 8 hours before draining and cutting into 2-inch pieces.

3. Assemble the hot pot ingredients by placing the dumplings, prepared bean curd stick, noodles, mushrooms, Chinese broccoli, tatsoi, spinach, pressed tofu, acorn squash, lotus root, and sweet potato on large plates and setting them on the table.

4. Set up the hot pot at the table and bring the pre-cooked broth to a boil over high heat.

5. Lay out the ingredients for the sauce bar, including the sesame sauce, and set the table with chopsticks, strainers, and other utensils.

6. Using chopsticks, a hot pot strainer, or tongs, lower your chosen ingredients into the hot broth. Once cooked through, remove from the broth and eat with your dipping sauces.

PAIRING TIP: If you are following Buddhist food prohibitions, then skip the beer and instead try a Chinese oolong or jasmine tea.

# VEGAN MANDARIN DUCK HOT POT

*Prep Time:* **35 MINUTES** *Make-Ahead Time:* **2 HOURS** *Makes* **4 SERVINGS** *Vegan*

This recipe is a Mandarin duck pot (yuān yāng, 鸳鸯) that includes two broths, one spicy and one mild. The Sichuan Green Ma La broth is not oily like the red version, so it goes better with leafy greens and tofu. Remember that spicy flavor compounds dissolve in oil, so both the Cilantro-Sesame Oil and the Ginger-Scallion Oil are not only flavorful but can help mute the heat.

**MAKE IN ADVANCE**

1 batch Mandarin Duck Clear
   Broth (page 39)

1 batch Sichuan Green Ma La
   Broth (page 40)

1 batch Cilantro-Sesame Oil
   (page 69)

1 batch Ginger-Scallion Oil
   (page 70)

12 Mushroom Dumplings
   (page 74)

6 ounces dried rice noodles

12 ounces fresh mushrooms
   (portobello, maitake,
   enoki, etc.)

8 ounces firm or extra-firm
   tofu, cut into 1-inch cubes

8 ounces fried bean curd

8 ounces fresh tofu skin, cut
   into 2-inch squares

8 ounces baby bok choy, cut
   into 1-inch strips

8 ounces Chinese cabbage,
   cut into 1-inch strips

8 ounces choy sum, cut into
   1-inch-wide pieces

1 large Yukon Gold potato, cut
   into ½-inch-thick discs

1 medium sweet potato, cut into
   ½-inch-thick discs

2 ears corn, cut into
   1-inch pieces

1. Prepare the broths, cilantro-sesame oil, ginger-scallion oil, and dumplings according to instructions.

2. In a large bowl, soak the noodles in hot water for 30 minutes, or according to package instructions. Set aside.

3. Assemble the hot pot ingredients by placing the dumplings, mushrooms, tofu, fried bean curd, tofu skin, bok choy, cabbage, choy sum, potato, sweet potato, and corn onto large plates and setting them on the table.

4. Set up the hot pot at the table and bring the broth to a boil over high heat. You'll need to either use a split hot pot or two individual hot pot setups.

5. Lay out the ingredients for the sauce bar, including the cilantro-sesame oil and ginger-scallion oil, and set the table with chopsticks, strainers, and other utensils.

6. When the broth comes to a boil, drain the noodles and transfer to a medium bowl to serve.

7. Using chopsticks, a hot pot strainer, or tongs, lower your chosen ingredients into the hot broth. Once cooked through, remove from the broth and eat with your dipping sauces.

PAIRING TIP: The light flavor of a pale lager like Tsingtao beer is a great accompaniment to a spicy broth.

# GUIZHOU DRAGON TOOTH HOT POT

*Prep Time:* **35 MINUTES** *Make-Ahead Time:* **3 HOURS, PLUS 8 HOURS TO PRE-SOAK**
*Makes* **4 SERVINGS** *Vegan*

This hot pot uses a regional broth from the Guizhou province that features pickled mustard greens. During my visit to Guizhou, I visited a rural elementary school in a small village located at the base of a dragon tooth mountain and surrounded by rice paddies. The horizon was a collection of triangular dragon tooth mountains like Chinese landscape paintings you've probably seen. As a child, I always thought these paintings were fantasy, but I now know they are real-life landscape paintings.

**MAKE IN ADVANCE**

1 batch Guizhou Pickled Greens and Bean Broth (page 44)

1 batch Cilantro-Sesame Oil (page 69)

12 Mushroom Dumplings (page 74)

2 to 3 ounces dried bean curd stick

4 ounces dried tofu knots

16 ounces firm or extra-firm tofu, cut into 1-inch cubes

16 ounces fresh wonton noodles

12 ounces fresh mushrooms (shiitake, shimeji, oyster, etc.)

¼ small sugar pumpkin (about 8 to 12 ounces), cut into 1-inch cubes

8 ounces bok choy, cut into 1-inch strips

8 ounces choy sum, cut into 1-inch-wide pieces

1 medium peeled lotus root, cut into ½-inch-thick discs

1. Prepare the broth, cilantro-sesame oil, and dumplings according to instructions.

2. In a 9-by-13-inch casserole dish, soak the bean curd stick in cool water. Cover and allow to soak for at least 8 hours before draining and cutting into 2-inch pieces.

3. In a medium bowl, soak the tofu knots in water for 20 minutes.

4. Assemble the hot pot ingredients by placing the dumplings, tofu, noodles, mushrooms, pumpkin, bok choy, choy sum, and lotus root on large plates and setting them on the table.

5. Set up the hot pot at the table and bring the pre-cooked broth to a boil over high heat.

6. Lay out the ingredients for the sauce bar, including the cilantro-sesame oil, and set the table with chopsticks, strainers, and other utensils.

7. When the broth comes to a boil, drain the bean curd stick and tofu knots and transfer to medium bowls to serve.

8. Using chopsticks, a hot pot strainer, or tongs, lower your chosen ingredients into the hot broth. Once cooked through, remove from the broth and eat with your dipping sauces.

PAIRING TIP: A farmhouse ale (also called Belgian saison) has a refreshing, citrusy flavor. Pale to golden-colored, the farmhouse ale has a medium body and citrus that will stand up to and complement the sourness of the broth.

# TOMATO BROTH HOT POT

*Prep Time:* **35 MINUTES** *Make-Ahead Time:* **1 HOUR 30 MINUTES, PLUS 8 HOURS TO PRE-SOAK** *Makes* **4 SERVINGS** *Vegan*

A tomato broth hot pot is a simple way to bring a savory flavor to your ingredients. This is one of the few ubiquitous uses of tomatoes in Chinese cuisine. Interestingly, one of our most common uses of tomatoes, ketchup, originated as a Chinese condiment. First brought back by British sailors as a fermented fish sauce more like today's Worcestershire sauce, it has evolved into the tomato-based condiment found in many American households.

### MAKE IN ADVANCE

1 batch Tomato Broth (page 62)

1 batch Jeff's Hot and Sour Dipping Sauce (page 72)

12 Mushroom Dumplings (page 74)

2 to 3 ounces dried bean curd stick

6 ounces dried mung bean (glass) noodles

16 ounces firm or extra-firm tofu, cut into 1-inch cubes

12 ounces fresh mushrooms (shiitake, enoki, wood ear, etc.)

8 ounces fried bean curd

8 ounces Chinese cabbage, cut into 1-inch strips

8 ounces baby bok choy, cut into 1-inch strips

1 large Yukon Gold potato, cut into ½-inch discs

1 medium peeled taro root, cut into ½-inch discs

1 small butternut squash, cut into 1-inch cubes

1. Prepare the broth, hot and sour dipping sauce, and dumplings according to instructions.

2. In a 9-by-13-inch casserole dish, soak the bean curd stick in cool water. Cover and allow to soak for at least 8 hours before draining and cutting into 2-inch pieces.

3. In a large bowl, soak the noodles in warm water for 15 minutes, or until pliable. Set aside.

4. Assemble the hot pot ingredients by placing the dumplings, tofu, mushrooms, fried bean curd, cabbage, bok choy, potato, taro root, and squash on large plates and setting them on the table.

5.  Set up the hot pot at the table and bring the pre-cooked broth to a boil over high heat.

6.  Lay out the ingredients for the sauce bar, including the hot and sour sauce, and set the table with chopsticks, strainers, and other utensils.

7.  When the broth comes to a boil, drain the noodles and transfer to medium bowls to serve.

8.  Using chopsticks, a hot pot strainer, or tongs, lower your chosen ingredients into the hot broth. Once cooked through, remove from the broth and eat with your dipping sauces.

PAIRING TIP: A Pilsner introduces a slight bitterness that helps balance the bright, acidic tomato broth.

# SPICY TOMATO YUĀN YĀNG HOT POT

*Prep Time:* **30 MINUTES**  *Make-Ahead Time:* **2 HOURS 30 MINUTES**
*Makes* **4 SERVINGS**  *Vegan*

One common dual hot pot combination is the classic spicy Sichuan Red Ma La Broth (page 38) and mild Tomato Broth (page 62). This version switches the spicy to the tomato broth and pairs it with the simple Mandarin Duck Clear Broth. The spicy tomato broth is less intense than the other spicy broths and is a good starter for those less accustomed to the heat!

**MAKE IN ADVANCE**

1 batch Sichuan Spicy Tomato Broth (page 41)

1 batch Mandarin Duck Clear Broth (page 39)

1 batch Jeff's Hot and Sour Sauce (page 72)

12 Mushroom Dumplings (see page 74)

8 ounces dried tofu knots

16 ounces firm or extra-firm tofu, cut into 1-inch cubes

8 ounces fresh tofu skin, cut into 2-inch squares

8 ounces Chinese broccoli, cut into 1-inch pieces

8 ounces bok choy, cut into 1-inch strips

8 ounces tatsoi, cut into 1-inch pieces

8 ounces fresh mushrooms (king trumpet, oyster, etc.)

1 large Yukon Gold potato, cut into ½-inch discs

8 ounces daikon radish, cut into 1-inch cubes

1 medium peeled lotus root, cut into ½-inch-thick discs

16 ounces fresh tofu noodles

1. Prepare the broths, hot and sour dipping sauce, and dumplings according to instructions.

2. In a medium bowl, soak the tofu knots in water for 20 minutes.

3. Assemble the hot pot ingredients by placing the dumplings, tofu, tofu skin, Chinese broccoli, bok choy, tatsoi, mushrooms, potato, daikon radish, lotus root, and noodles on large plates and setting them on the table.

4.  Set up the hot pot at the table and bring the broth to a boil over high heat. You'll need to use either a split hot pot or two individual hot pot setups.

5.  Lay out the ingredients for the sauce bar, including the hot and sour dipping sauce, and set the table with chopsticks, strainers, and other utensils.

6.  When the broth comes to a boil, drain the tofu knots and transfer to a medium bowl to serve.

7.  Using chopsticks, a hot pot strainer, or tongs, lower your chosen ingredients into the hot broth. Once cooked through, remove from the broth and eat with your dipping sauces.

PAIRING TIP: A Pilsner introduces a slight bitterness that helps balance the bright, acidic tomato broth.

INGREDIENT TIP: To allow the tofu to absorb more broth and flavor, compress it using a weight to squeeze out its liquid before cutting into cubes. To press out even more water, freeze the tofu in its original packaging; then defrost and compress.

*Hainan Island Hot Pot , page 116*

# CHAPTER SIX

# Meat and Seafood Hot Pots

Like in chapter 5, these recipes are suggested pairing lists rather than conventional recipes. Let your personal tastes and the availability of ingredients guide you. Feel free to substitute one leafy green vegetable or one protein for another. What's most important is to have a mix of proteins, leafy vegetables, and starches to provide balance. Dipping sauces should be personal, too, so try my suggestions, but also make up your own creation! See chapter 5 for more tips for your hot pot meal.

# NORTHERN YUĀN YĀNG HOT POT

*Prep Time:* **45 MINUTES** *Make-Ahead Time:* **3 HOURS, PLUS 8 HOURS TO PRE-SOAK**
*Makes* **4 SERVINGS**

This classic yuān yāng hot pot combines a spicy Sichuan broth with a simple clear broth. Capsaicin, the chemical responsible for the spiciness of chili peppers, is fat-soluble. Sesame paste and sesame oil are often paired with spicy broths and can help dissolve capsaicin. In Sichuan province, a bottle of sesame oil is as ubiquitous at hot pot as ketchup is at an American burger joint.

**MAKE IN ADVANCE**

1 batch Sichuan Red Ma La Broth (page 38)

1 batch Heilongjiang Clear Broth (page 50)

1 batch Cilantro-Sesame Oil (page 69)

1 batch Sesame Sauce (page 68)

8 Xinjiang Lamb Dumplings (page 78)

2 to 3 ounces dried bean curd stick

16 ounces fresh lo mein noodles

8 ounces spinach

8 ounces Chinese cabbage, cut into 1-inch strips

8 ounces fresh mushrooms (cremini, wood ear, etc.)

1 medium peeled lotus root, cut into ½-inch-thick discs

½ small acorn squash (8 to 12 ounces), cut into cubes

8 ounces rib-eye steak, thinly sliced

8 ounces beef short rib, thinly sliced

8 ounce beef tripe, thinly sliced

8 Chinese beef meatballs

1. Prepare the broths, cilantro-sesame oil, sesame sauce, and dumplings according to instructions.

2. In a 9-by-13 inch casserole dish, soak the bean curd stick in cool water. Cover and allow to soak for at least 8 hours before draining and cutting into 2-inch pieces.

3. Assemble the hot pot ingredients by placing the noodles, spinach, cabbage, mushrooms, lotus root, and acorn squash on plates and setting them on the table. Keep the dumplings, steak, short rib, tripe, and meatballs refrigerated until right before the meal.

4.  Set up the hot pot at the table and bring the broth to a boil over high heat. You'll need to use either a split hot pot or two individual hot pot setups.

5.  Lay out the ingredients for the sauce bar, including the cilantro-sesame oil and sesame sauce, and set the table with chopsticks, strainers, and other utensils.

6.  Using chopsticks, a hot pot strainer, or tongs, lower your chosen ingredients into the hot broth. Once cooked through, remove from the broth and eat with your dipping sauces.

PAIRING TIP: For more heat, go for an India pale ale (IPA). Its higher alcohol content and bitter notes are known to enhance the spiciness. If you don't want to compound the burning in your mouth, try a Bohemian pilsner.

# DABANJI HOT POT

*Prep Time:* **45 MINUTES** *Make-Ahead Time:* **2 HOURS 15 MINUTES** *Makes* **4 SERVINGS**

Celebrate one of western China's iconic dishes, DaBanJi, or "big plate chicken," with this hot pot combination. The beer-braised chicken and the broth owe much of their flavor to Xinjiang province's Wusu beer. Now owned by the Danish beer company Carlsberg, Wusu beers are becoming more available in the United States.

**MAKE IN ADVANCE**

1 batch Xinjiang DaBanJi Broth (page 58) and reserved cooked wings and thighs

1 batch Ginger-Scallion Oil (page 70)

1 batch Sesame Sauce (page 68)

8 Xinjiang Lamb Dumplings (page 78)

6 ounces dried mung bean (glass) noodles

4 ounces fresh bean curd skin, cut into 2-inch squares

8 ounces tatsoi, cut into 1-inch pieces

4 ounces shimeji mushrooms

2 green bell peppers, cut into 1-inch pieces

2 large carrots, cut on the bias into ¼-inch-thick pieces

1 large peeled potato, cut into ½-inch-thick discs

8 ounces brisket, thinly sliced

8 ounces rib-eye steak, thinly sliced

8 ounces beef tongue, thinly sliced

8 Chinese beef meatballs

1. Prepare the broth, ginger-scallion oil, sesame sauce, and dumplings according to instructions.

2. In a large bowl, soak the noodles in warm water for 15 minutes, or until pliable. Set aside.

3. Assemble the hot pot ingredients by placing the bean curd skin, tatsoi, mushrooms, bell peppers, carrots, and potato on plates and setting them on the table. Keep the dumplings, brisket, steak, tongue, meatballs, and cooked chicken refrigerated until right before the meal.

4. Set up the hot pot at the table and bring the pre-cooked broth to a boil over high heat.

5. Lay out the ingredients for the sauce bar, including the ginger-scallion oil and sesame sauce, and set the table with chopsticks, strainers, and other utensils.

6. When the broth comes to a boil, drain the noodles and transfer to a medium bowl to serve.

7. Using chopsticks, a hot pot strainer, or tongs, lower your chosen ingredients into the hot broth. Once cooked through, remove from the broth and eat with your dipping sauces.

**PAIRING TIP:** Xinjiang Wusu Black Beer or an amber or brown ale will complement the strong flavors of the broth and meats.

# NORTHERN BEEF AND LAMB HOT POT

*Prep Time:* **45 MINUTES** *Make-Ahead Time:* **2 HOURS** *Makes* **4 SERVINGS**

Lamb and mutton are more commonly consumed in Chinese cuisine, especially in northern China, than they are in the United States. In many northern regions including Beijing, lamb is often a central focus of the hot pot experience. This duo combines lamb and beef to accommodate the availability of beef products in the United States with the tradition of lamb in China.

**MAKE IN ADVANCE**

1 batch Mandarin Lamb Broth (page 49)

1 batch Sesame Sauce (page 68)

Sichuan Chili Oil (page 71)

12 Xinjiang Lamb Dumplings (page 78)

6 ounces dried rice noodles

8 ounces firm or extra-firm tofu, cut into 1-inch cubes

8 ounces dwarf bok choy, halved lengthwise

8 ounces Chinese broccoli, cut into 1-inch strips

8 ounces fresh mushrooms (button, wood ear, etc.)

1 medium sweet potato, cut into ½-inch-thick discs

1 medium peeled taro root, cut into ½-inch discs

8 ounces brisket, thinly sliced

8 ounces beef short rib, thinly sliced

8 ounces lamb shoulder, thinly sliced

8 ounces shrimp, peeled and deveined

4 ounces beef liver, thick-cut and crosshatched

1. Prepare the broth, sesame sauce, chili oil, and dumplings according to instructions.

2. In a large bowl, soak the noodles in hot water for 30 minutes, or according to package instructions. Set aside.

3. Assemble the hot pot ingredients by placing the tofu, bok choy, Chinese broccoli, mushrooms, sweet potato, and taro root on plates and setting them on the table. Keep the dumplings, brisket, short rib, lamb shoulder, shrimp, and liver refrigerated until right before the meal.

4. Set up the hot pot at the table and bring the pre-cooked broth to a boil over high heat.

5. Lay out the ingredients for the sauce bar, including the sesame sauce and chili oil, and set the table with chopsticks, strainers, and other utensils.

6. When the broth comes to a boil, drain the noodles and transfer to a medium bowl to serve.

7. Using chopsticks, a hot pot strainer, or tongs, lower your chosen ingredients into the hot broth. Once cooked through, remove from the broth and eat with your dipping sauces.

PAIRING TIP: An English brown ale's malty full-bodied flavor complements this meat-forward hot pot.

INGREDIENT TIP: To allow the tofu to absorb more broth and flavor, compress it using a weight to squeeze out its liquid before cutting into cubes. To press out even more water, freeze the tofu in its original packaging; then defrost and compress.

# CANTONESE HOT POT

*Prep Time:* **30 MINUTES** *Make-Ahead Time:* **1 HOUR 45 MINUTES** *Makes* **4 SERVINGS**

Cantonese cuisine is the cuisine of southern China and the Guangdong province. It is the most common style of Chinese food found in the United States since most of the early immigrants from China were from Guangdong province. Cantonese cuisine is light and sometimes slightly sweet, allowing you to taste the ingredients, as opposed to the more heavily sauced Sichuan cuisine where the dominant flavor is sometimes a fermented bean sauce. This hot pot combination will allow you to enjoy each ingredient's unique flavor.

**MAKE IN ADVANCE**

1 batch Cantonese Pork Bone Broth (page 52)

1 batch Cilantro-Sesame Oil (page 69)

12 Shrimp Paste Balls (page 79)

8 Pork and Shrimp Dumplings (page 76)

6 ounces dried rice noodles

8 ounces bok choy, cut into 1-inch strips

8 ounces spinach

8 ounces fresh mushrooms (enoki, shiitake, etc.)

6 ounces pressed tofu, cut into bite-size pieces

1 medium sweet potato, cut into ½-inch-thick discs

1 small butternut squash, cut into 1-inch cubes

8 ounces pork belly, thinly sliced

8 ounces Chinese lap cheong sausage, sliced on the bias into ¼-inch-thick pieces

8 ounces pork tripe, thinly sliced

1. Prepare the broth, cilantro-sesame oil, shrimp paste balls, and dumplings according to instructions.

2. In a large bowl, soak the noodles in hot water for 30 minutes, or according to package instructions. Set aside.

3. Assemble the hot pot ingredients by placing the bok choy, spinach, mushrooms, tofu, sweet potato, and squash on plates and setting them on the table. Keep the shrimp paste balls, dumplings, pork belly, sausage, and tripe refrigerated until right before the meal.

4.  Set up the hot pot at the table and bring the pre-cooked broth to a boil over high heat.

5.  Lay out the ingredients for the sauce bar, including the cilantro-sesame oil, and set the table with chopsticks, strainers, and other utensils.

6.  When the broth comes to a boil, drain the noodles and transfer to a medium bowl to serve.

7.  Using chopsticks, a hot pot strainer, or tongs, lower your chosen ingredients into the hot broth. Once cooked through, remove from the broth and eat with your dipping sauces.

PAIRING TIP: A sour beer like Flanders red ale or an American sour goes well with the fattiness of the pork belly and Chinese sausage.

# RUBY'S HOLIDAY HOT POT

*Prep Time:* **35 MINUTES** *Make-Ahead Time:* **1 HOUR 15 MINUTES** *Makes* **4 SERVINGS**

This hot pot is an homage to my grandmother Ruby, who hosted many family hot pot dinners, especially around the Christmas and New Year's holidays. The Spam in this recipe represents the leftover ham or turkey from those gatherings. She also always had sliced kielbasa sausage. Although not all of these ingredients are Chinese, this hot pot is a great way to enjoy the company of loved ones.

**MAKE IN ADVANCE**

1 batch Hunan Cured Meat Broth (page 48) and reserved cooked daikon radish

1 batch Jeff's Hot and Sour Dipping Sauce (page 72)

12 Xinjiang Lamb Dumplings (page 78)

16 ounces fresh lo mein noodles

8 ounces firm or extra-firm tofu, cut into 1-inch cubes

8 ounces Chinese cabbage, cut into 1-inch strips

8 ounces tatsoi, cut into 1-inch pieces

8 ounces fresh mushrooms (maitake, enoki, etc.)

1 medium peeled lotus root, cut into ½-inch-thick discs

1 (12-ounce) can Spam, cut into ¾-inch cubes

8 ounces pork loin, thinly sliced

8 ounces pork belly, thinly sliced

8 ounces kielbasa sausage, sliced on the bias into ¼-inch-thick pieces

1. Prepare the broth, hot and sour dipping sauce, and dumplings according to instructions.

2. Assemble the hot pot ingredients by placing the noodles, tofu, cabbage, tatsoi, mushrooms, and lotus root on plates and setting them on the table. Keep the dumplings, Spam, pork loin, pork belly, and sausage refrigerated until right before the meal.

3. Set up the hot pot at the table and bring the broth and daikon radish to a boil over high heat.

4. Lay out the ingredients for the sauce bar, including the hot and sour sauce, and set the table with chopsticks, strainers, and other utensils.

5. When the broth comes to a boil, bring out the refrigerated ingredients.

6. Using chopsticks, a hot pot strainer, or tongs, lower your chosen ingredients into the hot broth. Once cooked through, remove from the broth and eat with your dipping sauces.

PAIRING TIP: An American porter's strong malty sweetness and smoothness will complement the smoky and salty flavors from the cured and smoked meats.

INGREDIENT TIP: To allow the tofu to absorb more broth and flavor, compress it using a weight to squeeze out its liquid before cutting into cubes. To press out even more water, freeze the tofu in its original packaging; then defrost and compress.

# WEEKNIGHT HOT POT

*Prep Time:* **35 MINUTES**  *Make-Ahead Time:* **45 MINUTES**  *Makes* **4 SERVINGS**

The Heilongjiang Clear Broth is supposed to allow you to taste the ingredients you are cooking rather than the broth. Its simplicity also lets you pull together this entire hot pot in a relatively short time. If you have dumplings already made in the freezer, you could be starting your hot pot in as much time as it takes you to prep your ingredients and set the table.

**MAKE IN ADVANCE**

1 batch Heilongjiang Clear Broth (page 50)

1 batch Cilantro-Sesame Oil (page 69)

12 Pork and Shrimp Dumplings (page 76)

1 pound live clams or other shellfish (see page 33)

16 ounces fresh wonton noodles

8 ounces spinach

8 ounces Chinese broccoli, cut into 1-inch strips

¼ small sugar pumpkin (about 8 to 12 ounces), cut into 1-inch cubes

1 medium peeled taro root, cut into ½-inch discs

6 ounces pressed tofu, cut into bite-size pieces

4 ounces fresh shiitake mushrooms

8 ounces pork belly, thinly sliced

8 Chinese pork meatballs

8 fish balls

1.  Prepare the broth, cilantro-sesame oil, and dumplings according to instructions.

2.  Place the clams in a large bowl and keep cold in the refrigerator.

3.  Assemble the hot pot ingredients by placing the noodles, spinach, Chinese broccoli, pumpkin, taro root, tofu, and mushrooms on plates and setting them on the table. Keep the dumplings, pork belly, meatballs, and fish balls refrigerated until right before the meal.

4.  Set up the hot pot at the table and bring the pre-cooked broth to a boil over high heat.

5. Lay out the ingredients for the sauce bar, including the cilantro-sesame oil, and set the table with chopsticks, strainers, and other utensils.

6. When the broth comes to a boil, bring out the refrigerated ingredients.

7. Using chopsticks, a hot pot strainer, or tongs, lower your chosen ingredients into the hot broth. Once cooked through, remove from the broth and eat with your dipping sauces.

PAIRING TIP: A Belgian white is a light and refreshing beer with a slight citrus flavor that won't overwhelm the flavors of the food.

# THE ADMIRALS' BANQUET HOT POT

*Prep Time:* **45 MINUTES** *Make-Ahead Time:* **1 HOUR 30 MINUTES, PLUS 8 HOURS TO PRE-SOAK** *Makes* **4 SERVINGS**

My great-great-grandfather Wei Han and great-grandfather Mao Zhong-Fang and his two brothers were all admirals in the Chinese navy. Their service spanned from the Qing dynasty to the Chinese Republic. This hot pot combines many of my favorite foods, including lobster from my home in Maine and the Fujian Seafood Broth inspired by Fujian cuisine where my family has lived for over 500 years.

### MAKE IN ADVANCE

1 batch Fujian Seafood Broth (page 56) and reserved cooked lobster or crabmeat

1 batch Cilantro-Sesame Oil (page 69)

12 Pork and Shrimp Dumplings (page 76)

2 to 3 ounces dried bean curd stick

6 ounces dried rice noodles

8 ounces Chinese cabbage, cut into 1-inch strips

8 ounces baby bok choy, cut into 1-inch strips

4 ounces fresh shimeji mushrooms

2 ears corn, cut into 1-inch pieces

1 small daikon radish

12 ounces sea bass, sliced on the bias into ¼-inch-thick pieces

8 ounces shrimp, peeled and deveined

8 fish balls

1. Prepare the broth, cilantro-sesame oil, and dumplings according to instructions.

2. In a 9-by-13-inch casserole dish, soak the bean curd stick in cool water. Cover and soak for at least 8 hours before draining and cutting into 2-inch pieces.

3. In a large bowl, soak the noodles in hot water for 30 minutes, or according to package instructions. Set aside.

4. Assemble the hot pot ingredients by placing the cabbage, bok choy, mushrooms, corn, and daikon radish on plates and setting them on the table. Keep the dumplings, sea bass, shrimp, fish balls, and cooked lobster or crabmeat refrigerated until right before the meal.

5. Set up the hot pot at the table and bring the broth to a boil over high heat.

6. Lay out the ingredients for the sauce bar, including the cilantro-sesame oil, and set the table with chopsticks, strainers, and other utensils.

7. When the broth comes to a boil, drain the noodles and transfer to a medium bowl to serve.

8. Using chopsticks, a hot pot strainer, or tongs, lower your chosen ingredients into the hot broth. Once cooked through, remove from the broth and eat with your dipping sauces.

SUBSTITUTION TIP: You can alter the ratio of pork to shrimp in the dumpling filling. For this hot pot, try a 1:2 ratio of pork to shrimp rather than the 2:1 ratio in the recipe.

PAIRING TIP: A Belgian witbier or American wheat beer is a classic pairing with lobster. Lemony with a hint of coriander, wheat beers are often cloudy, not clear. I like Allagash White from Allagash Brewing in Portland, Maine.

# MAZU'S OCEAN FEAST HOT POT

*Prep Time:* **45 MINUTES** *Make-Ahead Time:* **1 HOUR 15 MINUTES** *Makes* **4 SERVINGS**

Legends say that Mazu was a real woman who lived from 960 to 987 CE. Born on Meizhou Island, Fujian province, she is worshipped as a goddess and considered a protector of fishermen and sailors by coastal populations and many Taiwanese. Many of Taiwan's earliest residents came from Fujian.

## MAKE IN ADVANCE

1 batch Cantonese Congee Broth (page 51)

1 batch Chile-Lime Sauce (page 73)

12 Pork and Shrimp Dumplings (page 76)

4 ounces dried tofu knots

1 pound live clams or other shellfish (see page 33)

16 ounces fresh lo mein noodles

8 ounces fresh mushrooms (wood ear, king trumpet, etc.)

6 ounces spinach

6 ounces tatsoi, cut into 1-inch pieces

6 ounces Chinese cabbage, cut into 1-inch strips

1 medium peeled lotus root, cut into ½-inch-thick discs

12 ounces cod or haddock, sliced on the bias into ¼-inch-thick pieces

8 ounces shrimp, peeled and deveined

8 ounces squid, cut into 2-inch squares and crosshatched

1. Prepare the broth, chile-lime sauce, and dumplings according to instructions.

2. In a medium bowl, soak the tofu knots in water for 20 minutes.

3. Prepare the shellfish, place in a large bowl, and keep cold in the refrigerator.

4. Assemble the hot pot ingredients by placing the noodles, mushrooms, spinach, tatsoi, cabbage, and lotus root on plates and setting them on the table. Keep the dumplings, cod, shrimp, and squid refrigerated until right before the meal.

5. Set up the hot pot at the table and bring the pre-cooked broth to a boil over high heat.

6. Lay out the ingredients for the sauce bar, including the chile-lime sauce, and set the table with chopsticks, strainers, and other utensils.

7. When the broth comes to a boil, drain the tofu knots and transfer to a medium bowl to serve.

8. Using chopsticks, a hot pot strainer, or tongs, lower your chosen ingredients into the hot broth. Once cooked through, remove from the broth and eat with your dipping sauces.

SUBSTITUTION TIP: Try substituting ground chicken for the ground pork in the dumpling filling. You can also add ¼ cup of diced water chestnuts if you like a little crunch.

PAIRING TIP: A farmhouse ale (also called Belgian saison) has a refreshing, zesty, and citrusy flavor. Pale to golden-colored farmhouse ales go well with seafood.

# GUIZHOU FISHERMAN'S HOT POT

*Prep Time:* **35 MINUTES** *Make-Ahead Time:* **1 HOUR 30 MINUTES** *Makes* **4 SERVINGS**

The broth for this hot pot is flavored both by poaching the fish in the broth and from pickled sour mustard greens. The preparation of the broth will result in a good portion of cooked fish to kick-start your meal.

**MAKE IN ADVANCE**

1 batch Guizhou Sour Fish Broth (page 42) and reserved cooked fish

1 batch Ginger-Scallion Oil (page 70)

12 Shrimp Paste Balls (page 79)

12 Pork and Shrimp Dumplings (page 76)

1 pound clams or other shellfish

16 ounces fresh lo mein noodles

8 ounces fried bean curd

8 ounces choy sum, cut into 1-inch-wide pieces

8 ounces Chinese cabbage, cut into 1-inch strips

4 ounces fresh shimeji mushrooms

1 medium sweet potato, cut into ½-inch-thick discs

2 ears corn, cut into 1-inch pieces

1. Prepare the broth, ginger-scallion oil, shrimp paste balls, and dumplings according to instructions.

2. Prepare the shellfish, place in a large bowl, and keep cold in the refrigerator.

3. Assemble the hot pot ingredients by placing the noodles, fried bean curd, choy sum, cabbage, mushrooms, sweet potato, corn, and reserved cooked fish on plates and setting them on the table. Keep the shrimp paste balls and dumplings refrigerated until right before the meal.

4. Set up the hot pot at the table and bring the pre-cooked broth to a boil over high heat.

5. Lay out the ingredients for the sauce bar, including the ginger-scallion oil, and set the table with chopsticks, strainers, and other utensils.

6. When the broth comes to a boil, set out the refrigerated ingredients.

7. Using chopsticks, a hot pot strainer, or tongs, lower your chosen ingredients into the hot broth. Once cooked through, remove from the broth and eat with your dipping sauces.

PAIRING TIP: A medium-bodied German or Belgian Lager is robust enough to stand up to the sourness of the broth.

# HAINAN ISLAND HOT POT

*Prep Time:* **35 MINUTES** *Make-Ahead Time:* **1 HOUR 15 MINUTES** *Makes* **4 SERVINGS**

The hot pot combination brings a uniquely tropical flavor profile from the coconut water used in the broth along with the chile-lime sauce that is commonly paired with Hainan chicken. It also will include poached chicken from the broth preparation, which you can heat in the broth or eat at room temperature.

**MAKE IN ADVANCE**

1 batch Hainan Chicken-Coconut Broth (page 53) and reserved poached chicken

1 batch Chile-Lime Sauce (page 73)

12 Pork and Shrimp Dumplings (page 76)

16 ounces fresh lo mein noodles

8 ounces baby bok choy, cut into 1-inch strips

8 ounces choy sum, cut into 1-inch-wide pieces

8 ounces fresh mushrooms (enoki, wood ear, etc.)

½ small kabocha squash (about 8 to 12 ounces), cut into 1-inch cubes

6 ounces pressed tofu, cut into bite-size pieces

4 ounces fresh bean curd skin

8 ounces shrimp, peeled and deveined

8 Chinese pork meatballs

1. Prepare the broth, chile-lime sauce, and dumplings according to instructions.

2. Assemble the hot pot ingredients by placing the noodles, bok choy, choy sum, mushrooms, squash, tofu, bean curd skin, and reserved poached chicken on plates and setting them on the table. Keep the dumplings, shrimp, and meatballs refrigerated until right before the meal.

3. Set up the hot pot at the table and bring the pre-cooked broth to a boil over high heat.

4. Lay out the ingredients for the sauce bar, including the chile-lime sauce, and set the table with chopsticks, strainers, and other utensils.

5.  When the broth comes to a boil, set out the refrigerated ingredients.

6.  Using chopsticks, a hot pot strainer, or tongs, lower your chosen ingredients into the hot broth. Once cooked through, remove from the broth and eat with your dipping sauces.

SUBSTITUTION TIP: You can substitute ground chicken for the ground pork in the Pork and Shrimp Dumplings recipe.

PAIRING TIP: The hoppy and citrus notes from an India pale ale, along with a strong bitterness, provide a nice contrast to the sweetness of the coconut-infused broth and complement the chile-lime sauce.

# DRUNKEN CHICKEN HOT POT

*Prep Time:* **35 MINUTES** *Make-Ahead Time:* **1 HOUR 30 MINUTES** *Makes* **4 SERVINGS**

Zhejiang province is relatively small, covering a landmass just a bit larger than my home state of Maine, but its population is over 54 million. At various times, it was home to the nation's capital. Its cuisine is therefore descended from the royal court and emphasizes health and long life, often incorporating traditional Chinese medicinal herbs like those in the Zhejiang Drunken Chicken Broth.

**MAKE IN ADVANCE**

1 batch Zhejiang Drunken Chicken Broth (page 55)

1 batch Cilantro-Sesame Oil (page 69)

12 Shrimp Paste Balls (page 79)

8 Pork and Shrimp Dumplings (page 76)

16 ounces fresh wonton noodles

8 ounces firm or extra-firm tofu, cut into 1-inch cubes

8 ounces Chinese cabbage, cut into 1-inch strips

8 ounces Chinese broccoli, cut into 1-inch strips

8 ounces fresh mushrooms (maitake, button, etc.)

1 medium sweet potato, cut into ½-inch-thick discs

1 medium peeled lotus root, cut into ½-inch-thick discs

8 ounces skinless boneless chicken thighs, thinly sliced

8 ounces sea bass fillets, sliced on the bias into ¼-inch-thick pieces

1. Prepare the broth, cilantro-sesame oil, shrimp paste balls, and dumplings according to instructions.

2. Assemble the hot pot ingredients by placing the noodles, tofu, cabbage, Chinese broccoli, mushrooms, sweet potato, lotus root, and drunken chicken from the broth on plates and setting them on the table. Keep the shrimp paste balls, dumplings chicken thighs, and sea bass refrigerated until right before the meal.

3. Set up the hot pot at the table and bring the pre-cooked broth to a boil over high heat.

4. Lay out the ingredients for the sauce bar, including the cilantro-sesame oil, and set the table with chopsticks, strainers, and other utensils.

5.  When the broth comes to a boil, set out the refrigerated ingredients.

6.  Using chopsticks, a hot pot strainer, or tongs, lower your chosen ingredients into the hot broth. Once cooked through, remove from the broth and eat with your dipping sauces.

SUBSTITUTION TIP: You can substitute ground chicken for the ground pork in the Pork and Shrimp Dumplings recipe.

PAIRING TIP: An American pale wheat beer has a light crisp flavor and low alcohol content that will fit nicely with this "drunken" broth and not overpower the chicken and seafood.

# IMMORTALITY HOT POT

*Prep Time:* **35 MINUTES**  *Make-Ahead Time:* **1 HOUR 30 MINUTES**  *Makes* **4 SERVINGS**

The Empress Dowager Cixi of the Qing Dynasty made the chrysanthemum hot pot famous by incorporating it into her regimen to maintain long life and beauty. It was under her rule that my great-great-grandfather Wei Han went to Europe to learn Western technologies. He is credited as the father of the modern Chinese navy, having founded the Mawei Shipyard that built China's first iron ships in 1887. I don't know if he enjoyed this hot pot, but he has achieved practical immortality, as his likeness is now cast in bronze in a museum in Fuzhou.

**MAKE IN ADVANCE**

1 batch Chrysanthemum Blossom Broth (page 54) and reserved poached chicken

1 batch Ginger-Scallion Oil (page 70)

12 Pork and Shrimp Dumplings (page 76)

16 ounces fresh tofu noodles

8 chicken or quail eggs

8 ounces firm or extra-firm tofu, cut into 1-inch cubes

8 ounces baby bok choy, cut into 1-inch strips

8 ounces Chinese cabbage, cut into 1-inch strips

8 ounces fresh mushrooms (oyster, king trumpet, etc.)

1 small butternut squash, cut into 1-inch cubes

1 medium peeled taro root, cut into ½-inch discs

4 ounces rice stick

8 ounces pork belly, thinly sliced

8 ounces shrimp, peeled and deveined

1. Prepare the broth, ginger-scallion oil, and dumplings according to instructions.

2. Assemble the hot pot ingredients by placing the noodles, eggs, tofu, bok choy, cabbage, mushrooms, squash, taro root, rice stick, and reserved poached chicken on plates and setting them on the table. Keep the dumplings, pork belly, and shrimp refrigerated until right before the meal.

3. Set up the hot pot at the table and bring the pre-cooked broth to a boil over high heat.

4. Lay out the ingredients for the sauce bar, including the ginger-scallion oil, and set the table with chopsticks, strainers, and other utensils.

5. When the broth comes to a boil, set out the refrigerated ingredients.

6. Using chopsticks, a hot pot strainer, or tongs, lower your chosen ingredients into the hot broth. Once cooked through, remove from the broth and eat with your dipping sauces.

SUBSTITUTION TIP: You can substitute ground chicken for the ground pork in the Pork and Shrimp Dumplings recipe.

PAIRING TIP: An American lager has a light flavor and low alcohol content that will meld well with the floral yet light broth.

# SHEEP SCORPION HOT POT

*Prep Time:* **45 MINUTES**  *Make-Ahead Time:* **3 HOURS 30 MINUTES**  *Makes* **4 SERVINGS**

This style of hot pot is heavily laden with mutton and comes from Inner Mongolia. Legends trace its origins to the Naiman tribes whose members are now found from Inner Mongolia to central Asia.

**MAKE IN ADVANCE**

1 batch Sheep Scorpion Broth (page 60)

1 batch Cilantro-Sesame Oil (page 69)

12 Shrimp Paste Balls (page 79)

12 Xinjiang Lamb Dumplings (page 78)

4 ounces dried tofu knots

16 ounces fresh lo mein noodles

8 ounces dwarf bok choy, halved lengthwise

8 ounces tatsoi, cut into 1-inch pieces

8 ounces fresh mushrooms (wood ear, shiitake, etc.)

2 ears corn, cut into 1-inch pieces

1 large Yukon Gold potato

8 ounces lamb shoulder, thinly sliced

8 ounces lamb leg, thinly sliced

8 ounces pork belly, thinly sliced

1. Prepare the broth, cilantro-sesame oil, shrimp paste balls, and dumplings according to instructions.

2. In a medium bowl, soak the tofu knots in water for 20 minutes.

3. Assemble the hot pot ingredients by placing the noodles, bok choy, tatsoi, mushrooms, corn, and potato on plates and setting them on the table. Keep the shrimp paste balls, dumplings, lamb shoulder, lamb leg, and pork refrigerated until right before the meal.

4. Set up the hot pot and bring the pre-cooked broth to a boil over high heat.

5. Lay out the ingredients for the sauce bar, including the cilantro-sesame oil, and set the table with chopsticks, strainers, and other utensils.

6. When the broth comes to a boil, drain the tofu knots and transfer to a bowl to serve.

7. Using chopsticks, a hot pot strainer, or tongs, lower your chosen ingredients into the hot broth. Once cooked through, remove from the broth and eat with your dipping sauces.

PAIRING TIP: Xinjiang Wusu Black Beer or a malty medium- to full-bodied beer like an amber or brown ale will complement the strong flavors of this broth and the lamb.

# Measurement Conversions

## VOLUME EQUIVALENTS

| | U.S. STANDARD | U.S. STANDARD (OUNCES) | METRIC (APPROXIMATE) |
|---|---|---|---|
| **LIQUID** | 2 tablespoons | 1 fl. oz. | 30 mL |
| | ¼ cup | 2 fl. oz. | 60 mL |
| | ½ cup | 4 fl. oz. | 120 mL |
| | 1 cup | 8 fl. oz. | 240 mL |
| | 1½ cups | 12 fl. oz. | 355 mL |
| | 2 cups or 1 pint | 16 fl. oz. | 475 mL |
| | 4 cups or 1 quart | 32 fl. oz. | 1 L |
| | 1 gallon | 128 fl. oz. | 4 L |
| **DRY** | ⅛ teaspoon | | 0.5 mL |
| | ¼ teaspoon | | 1 mL |
| | ½ teaspoon | | 2 mL |
| | ¾ teaspoon | | 4 mL |
| | 1 teaspoon | | 5 mL |
| | 1 tablespoon | | 15 mL |
| | ¼ cup | | 59 mL |
| | ⅓ cup | | 79 mL |
| | ½ cup | | 118 mL |
| | ⅔ cup | | 156 mL |
| | ¾ cup | | 177 mL |
| | 1 cup | | 235 mL |
| | 2 cups or 1 pint | | 475 mL |
| | 3 cups | | 700 mL |
| | 4 cups or 1 quart | | 1 L |
| | ½ gallon | | 2 L |
| | 1 gallon | | 4 L |

## OVEN TEMPERATURES

| FAHRENHEIT | CELSIUS (APPROXIMATE) |
|---|---|
| 250°F | 120°C |
| 300°F | 150°C |
| 325°F | 165°C |
| 350°F | 180°C |
| 375°F | 190°C |
| 400°F | 200°C |
| 425°F | 220°C |
| 450°F | 230°C |

## WEIGHT EQUIVALENTS

| U.S. STANDARD | METRIC (APPROXIMATE) |
|---|---|
| ½ ounce | 15 g |
| 1 ounce | 30 g |
| 2 ounces | 60 g |
| 4 ounces | 115 g |
| 8 ounces | 225 g |
| 12 ounces | 340 g |
| 16 ounces or 1 pound | 455 g |

# Resources

"Food for Thought" Hot Pot episode from the *Culinary China* docuseries. (YouTu.be/cC19WuzK_fs). A 10-minute documentary about Sichuan hot pot including an interview with the woman who claims to have invented the split-pot hot pot.

HotPotAmbassador.com. A blog with lots of articles about hot pot, from history to helpful how-to articles.

KneadandNosh.com. My online home, where you'll find videos and other resources from me about hot pot and more!

TheMalaMarket.com. This site is a great source for Chinese chiles, Sichuan peppercorns, and other hot pot essentials.

"The ULTIMATE Chinese Food Tour: Pixian Broad Bean Paste in Chengdu" (YouTu.be/Y9pjr8--v8I). A five-minute video feature about Sichuan broad bean chili paste Píxiàn dòubàn jiàng.

*The Woks of Life* (TheWoksOfLife.com/chinese-hot-pot-at-home) is a great blog for Chinese recipes. This article includes helpful links to ingredient descriptions and photos. There's also a helpful guide, "How to Cut a Whole Chicken Chinese-style."

# References

Barron, James. "New York City's Population Hits a Record 8.6 Million." *New York Times*. March 22, 2018. NYTimes.com/2018/03/22/nyregion/new-york-city-population.html.

Food and Agriculture Organization of the United Nations. "FAOSTAT: Crops 2019 Data Set." Accessed May 26, 2021. FAO.org/faostat/en/#search/Crops%202019%20 Data%20Set.

Huang, Guanghong. "Chongqing Hotpot Festival! Thousands of People Share a Tasty Feast Together." *Chongqing Daily*. October 26, 2019. CQRB.cn/html/cqrb /2019-10/26/003/content_245240.htm.

People's Daily. "Hotpot, Barbecue Can Be Traced Back to China's Han Dynasty." Accessed May 10, 2021. en.People.cn/n3/2016/0525/c98649-9063044.html.

Statista. "Cities with the Largest Number of Starbucks in the United States as of April 2019." Accessed May 12, 2021. Statista.com/statistics/306896/cities-with -the-largest-number-of-starbucks-stores-us.

World Population Review. "Chongqing Population 2021." Accessed May 12, 2021. WorldPopulationReview.com/world-cities/chongqing-population.

Zhang, Tingwei. "Chinese Hotpot: A Communal Food Culture." December 23, 2019. StoryMaps.arcgis.com/stories/9c3a733c1411400e9f80310fa8b65a9e.

# Index

# ACKNOWLEDGMENTS

· · · · · · · · · · · · · · · · · · · ·

Thanks to my family, especially my wife, Deanna, and my sons, Peter and Nathan, for putting up with my recipe testing for years and years. My sister, Jennifer, and father were instrumental in aiding me with translating Chinese websites and texts and leveraging their many years living in China to ensure that I hadn't strayed too far from authentic hot pot.

A special thanks to Chris Toy. I met Chris almost 30 years ago as a young educator when he was a veteran school principal. A fellow Bowdoin College graduate, he guided me then, and he continues to do so now. He is the author of five Chinese cookbooks, and he encouraged me to create this book!

# ABOUT THE AUTHOR

· · · · · · · · · · · · · · · · · · · ·

 Jeff Mao (毛念宗) has been preparing Chinese food with his family since he was a child. His earliest cooking memories date back to the early 1970s, cutting and rolling Mandarin pancakes and filling and folding dumplings. He grew up outside San Francisco, and his childhood home had a black burnt circle on the kitchen peninsula where the family ate most of their meals—a scar from when his father accidentally placed the charcoal in the wrong place in their hot pot, cooking the counter more than heating the broth. A graduate of Tamalpais High School in Mill Valley, California, Mao moved to Maine to attend Bowdoin College, where he studied Russian history, played clarinet in the college's concert band, and ran on the track and field team. He has been an educator his entire professional career, but cooking has always remained a passion. Now an education technology consultant, Mao also teaches cooking classes online. You can find him at KneadAndNosh.com and EdMoxie.com.

CPSIA information can be obtained
at www.ICGtesting.com
Printed in the USA
JSHW011709301221
21597JS00001B/1